WAR, LOVE AND FAITH

STEPHEN AND JUDY UZELAC

BOOKS
ACADEMY
LEARNING LIFE FROM EVERY PAGE

BOOKS ACADEMY
LEARNING LIFE FROM EVERY PAGE

Copyright © 2025 by Stephen and Judy Uzelac

Books Academy LLC

112 SW HK Dodgen Loop,
Temple, Texas 76504

Hotline: (254) 800-1189

Ordering Information: Quantity sales. Special discounts are available on quantity purchases by corporations, associations, and others. For details, contact the publisher at the address above.

Printed in the United States of America.

ISBN: Softcover: 978-1-966567-97-4

            eBook :   978-1-966567-98-1

Library of Congress Control Number: 2025914060

TABLE OF CONTENTS

Vietnam War

Tommy T. Tucker, a United States Marine, writes a letter to Chi Le, his fiancée. However, Chi Le never received the letter.
My dearest Love - Chi,

My dearest Love - Chi,

I miss your beautiful face, gentle smile, and warm, lovely eyes. My heart longs for you! I eagerly wait for the day this unnecessary war ends, so we can snuggle in our small home together. Did you manage to fix the sink faucet? This war has been crazy, bloody, and brutal for everyone. I hope it ends soon so we can walk down the aisle hand in hand, with the gods from the mountaintops and our Jesus watching over us. Many lives have been lost. I saw things I didn't want anyone to see. It's like the American soldiers killing my ancestors and taking their land. So many innocent children, women, and young boys & girls are being killed, and I ask: For what? But I still see blessings, and you are my first blessing.

May an eagle soar and a fox rush to bring this letter to you!
With ever-ending love,
Triple T.

Chi Lee wrote a letter to Tommy, not knowing if he would ever receive it while he was fighting in Vietnam. Jungle.

Tommy, where are you?
I'm worried about my safety, so I believe I need to leave Saigon. I want to go back to the Christian home where I think I will be welcomed, but I'm still unsure if I'll be safe there. I need to find a place where I feel secure; right now, I don't know where that might be. I saw some terrible things that soldiers did to women on the street, and it has made me feel scared. I sincerely pray this letter reaches you and that you are safe and unharmed.
Your love truly is God's greatest blessing. I long to be in your warm embrace and share those precious, private moments. I dream of feeling your soft skin next to mine, holding me close; of the whispered promises we cherish. I eagerly listen to hear your footsteps and imagine your radiant smile as our eyes meet. I reach out for you in my dreams, only to find the emptiness there. I need to go now, but I pray that Jesus watches over you, and together we will walk through life. I must leave now. Loving you, I'll wait.

Chi

"We are merely transient visitors to this planet for no more than a century. During this period, we ought to endeavor to contribute positively to the lives of others. When helping others, you will discover the true meaning of life." Stephen Uzelac

Chi Le had to leave her comfortable home behind after a heartbreaking tragedy—she witnessed the loss of her parents. At just 12 years old, she embarks on a brave journey from her home to Saigon, navigating through the lush rice fields and dense jungle in search of Sister Mary. She doesn't know that her journey will lead her on a long, challenging path for many years.

Chapter 1
The Village

As the sun gradually sets behind the mountains and the streetlights illuminate the pathway, a tall, slender man with skin that reflects the sunlight approaches the Tavern.

The Tavern is the town's sole establishment, providing a hot meal and spirit. Attired in a long marine rain coat that reaches nearly to his ankles and a tan hat that obscures his face, he is Mr. Tommy T. Tucker, known among his limited circle of friends as Triple T.

Most villagers call him "The Stranger", despite his residence in the village for over 15 years. Mr. Tommy T. Tucker resides approximately a mile from the Tavern, situated along a private lane in the woods amidst evergreens, deer, black bears, and the occasional rattlesnake or mountain lion. The villagers possess scant knowledge regarding Triple T's background. Tommy established his residence in The Village around 1981 following his discharge from the Marine Corps in 1980.

Triple T. did not originate from the village; however, his grandfather bequeathed a mountain abundant with trees and wildlife. Some assert that the parcel encompasses over 60,000 acres, yet that is not all. He also inherited millions, accompanied by a message:

"Only use what you need and share what you have."

At the base of the mountain, a meadow gently descends into a stream that is excellent for trout fishing.

Tommy T. walks into the cozy tavern, making his way to a quiet table tucked away in the corner, away from the hustle and bustle. Rose, the friendly waitress, brings him a tall glass of Iron City beer, a drink he's been savoring for the past fifteen years.

Rose asks if he wants to try Friday night's special, Fish and Chips.

With a warm nod, Tommy happily agrees, though no further words are needed.

When his tab comes to $7.48, he leaves a ten-dollar bill along with two one-dollar bills, showing his appreciation with a tip that's over twenty percent.

Over the years, he has always been a generous tipper.

Each Christmas, he gave Rose a special five-hundred-dollar tip and generously tipped the cook, dishwasher, and other servers.

He and Rose mutually understood that he should keep his generosity between them, and she would make sure everyone received their share over the coming weeks.

This act of kindness holds a special place in Tommy's heart. He remembers Chi Le serving GIs at their table, always smiling even when they were obnoxious, rude, and downright ignorant.

Slowly, he rises from his table and heads towards the door, his gait reminiscent of John Wayne, complemented by friendly nods and a tip of his hat as he strolls through the tavern.

Most who patronized the Tavern eagerly watched as Tommy slowly approached the door. Once he stepped outside, his short smile and the cheerful lift of his brows became visible, signaling the start of his journey home.

On lovely days, Tommy enjoys a peaceful walk, while on rainy days or when the snow piles up, he hops into his trusty 1980 Ford truck.

Along the path home, you can hear dogs barking, crickets singing, and fish jumping in the creek. The village is a charming and peaceful place, home to the Tavern, two fly-fishing shops, three churches, an auto repair garage, and a cozy post office, making it an excellent spot to put down roots.

Once Tommy T. exits the Tavern, you can hear people talking.

Who is he? He frightens me! He sure is odd. He never talks to anyone, and the children are afraid of him.

Rose responds, "He is the best-looking man here, and he tips better than all of you. He came in here years ago, and have any of you welcomed him or tried to talk to him?"

They don't know Mr. Tommy T. Tucker, who received the Medal of Honor from President Jimmy Carter in 1980. The Medal of Honor is the highest U.S. military decoration, awarded to a member of the armed forces for gallantry and in combat at the risk of life above and beyond the call of duty.

Along with the Medal of Honor, Triple T. earned a Bronze Star for performing actions that show bravery and courage, along with the Purple Heart. The Purple Heart is a United States military medal awarded to those wounded or killed in the name of the President.

Tommy T. was wounded more than once and always got bandaged up and back to action as quickly as possible. His body looked like a pincushion.

Shortly after graduating from high school, Tommy joined the Marine Corps. At the age of seventeen, he graduated with honors in 1963.

He was born on November 5, 1940.

Master Gunnery Sergeant Tommy T. Tucker served in the United States Marine Corps for 20-plus years. His first assignment after boot camp at Recruit Depot Parris Island, South Carolina, was at Camp Geiger in North Carolina. This training included a 29-day infantry course through the School of Infantry.

Due to his size and knowledge, he became a drill instructor and was sent to the Recruit Depot in San Diego, California. In 1961, Tommy was assigned to a special unit and sent to Vietnam to study the situation and provide information on the actions of the Vietnamese military.

He soon discovered that Vietnam was a jungle, and most people in the south were likable; he began to appreciate their culture and food. Vietnam would be Tommy's final assignment. He stayed, and for over fifteen years, he fought in the war until the end of 1975.

Shortly after the war ended, Tommy was honorably discharged in 1981.

Toward the end of the war, Tommy's attitude began to shift. He was a proud American who loved the red, white, and blue, but he saw things he could not understand or accept. He felt that those serving Nam were sometimes forgotten and not treated equally, as evidenced by his friend being passed over for promotion because of the color of his skin. Tommy led his men on operations that lasted 30 days or more in some of Vietnam's most inhospitable conditions, "without shaving, bathing, or changing clothing."

Word began to filter back to the troops in Nam, who were at home and not receiving a hero's welcome. Returning GIs soon discovered that GI benefits available for Vietnam veterans "were almost nonexistent." "All that I went through in Nam," Tommy said, "None of that prepared me for the reception I received at home."

When I first arrived on the West Coast, I was in uniform and soon learned I was not welcome. It wasn't that I was a Native American; it was because I was a Marine.

Tommy T. was an orphan and foster child from an early age, starting at six, after the death of his parents. He went to live with his grandfather.

After his grandfather passed away, Tommy became a foster child until graduation.
Tommy has many beautiful memories of his Gramps: cutting and chopping firewood, hunting for dinner, planting a garden, picking mushrooms and herbs, and finding special pieces of wood for carving.

Once Gramps passed on, Tommy T. Tucker was placed in state custody, and with no family, he entered the foster system.

Early in his military career, he decided to commit to the Marines. The Vietnam War lasted from November 1, 1955, to April 30, 1975, officially between North Vietnam and South Vietnam. It was an international conflict that started with the French and later involved the United States and its allies supporting South Vietnam, against the Communist Bloc backing North Vietnam.

In Vietnam, Triple T was often seen carving figurines from wood blocks. Many of his carvings were given to his friend T.J. Jackson, who sent them to his father in NYC. Little did Tommy T. know that T.J.'s father was an art dealer in The Big Apple, who took a small commission and saved the rest in an account for Tommy T.

Tommy T. is deployed to Vietnam (1962)

- Initially, President Kennedy held back from sending combat troops; however, he approved the deployment of advisors and more soldiers. T.T. Tucker would serve as one of those advisors.

- Little did Tommy T. realize, just like many others, how profoundly this would alter his life.
- He acknowledged the conflict and the potential for a larger war yet maintained his commitment to the USA and the Marines. Tommy was raised to respect and honor the United States.

- The situation in Vietnam was viewed as an internal conflict, and corruption eroded Kennedy's confidence in the South Vietnamese government.

- Historians continue to debate whether Kennedy would have increased or reduced U.S. troop presence in Vietnam, with some arguing he might have favored a gradual withdrawal.

- President Kennedy increased the number of U.S. military advisors from about 700 to more than 16,000.

- At this time, most people were unaware of what was unfolding in Vietnam, better known as "Operation Beef Up."

- Kennedy set up this command to organize U.S. support for South Vietnam, aiming to encourage the government to implement political and social reforms to enhance its image and stability.

During his deployment in Vietnam, Tommy utilized the skills imparted to him by his grandfather to create intricate wooden art pieces suitable for exhibition in esteemed art museums globally. He carved over one hundred pieces, which were subsequently sent to T.J.'s father in New York City. The piece to the left was sold at auction for $1,500.00. Unbeknownst to Tommy T, he was on the path to fame. It is important to note that during this period in history, the internet did not exist.

Master Sergeant Tucker was invited to stay in Vietnam before shipping back to Camp Pendleton, Oceanside, California. After being discharged on the West Coast, Tommy visited his friend M.J. Fox in Los Angeles, where he acquired a 1980 Ford Truck, which, today, with nearly 300,000 miles, appears as if it is brand new. Tommy demonstrates care for his possessions.

Following this, Tommy drove across the country, stopping in Arizona, New Mexico, Texas, Louisiana, and Florida. He then proceeded north along Interstate 95 to New York City to visit his Marine friend, TJ Jackson.

While navigating 95 near Washington, D.C., Tommy contemplated stopping to see the President and share his insights. TJ and his family resided in a highly affluent neighborhood in West Harlem, featuring six bedrooms, six bathrooms, a five-car garage, a swimming pool, and ample living space. (It was uncommon for Black individuals to attain such wealth, yet TJ's father defied the prevailing stereotypes.) They also embodied the essence of commonality, as familiar as apple pie.

Tommy spent several days with the family and was greatly concerned about TJ, who exhibited symptoms of Post-Traumatic Stress Disorder (PTSD). The ramifications of the war were not favorable for TJ. Jackson had been awarded a Purple Heart for his service in Vietnam. Years later, he manifested symptoms of malaria, a tropical illness prevalent in urban environments. Nevertheless, he was denied Veterans Benefits and health care due to the absence of symptoms during his service in Vietnam.

Upon his departure from the military, Tommy accumulated considerable money within the military credit union, yielding an interest rate exceeding six percent. During his time in Vietnam, Tommy did not spend foolishly and could subsist on the military's provisions while stationed there. Consequently, he had more than $300,000 reserved for the unforeseen. The only money he spent was buying a small home for himself and Chi, and he got a stipend from the Marines for moving off base.

Tommy tends to be reticent and expresses little interest in listening to others as they vocalize their grievances regarding the weather, the lack of fish biting, and matters concerning our government.

To Tommy, the government represents another form of organized crime that siphons resources from the impoverished to benefit the affluent. He would prefer to embody Robin Hood's ideals.

As one approaches his residence, numerous No Trespassing signs become visible. His Ford truck is situated adjacent to his house. He has constructed his home and workshop using timber from his forest, with assistance from the nearby Amish community. Together, they successfully built a picturesque residence featuring a wrap-around porch, a kitchen with all essential appliances, a dining area, a living room, and three bathrooms.

Tommy's workshop is double the size of his residence and is connected to his home from the rear, facilitating seamless movement between his house and workspace. His office is in the workshop area, where he accommodates his IBM computer, electric typewriter, printer, TV, and efficient phone system that keeps him in close contact with friends and clients.

Currently, Triple T is in the process of finalizing a project with a client situated in New York City. The client has specifically requested a carved wall piece for his office on Wall Street. Walnut would be the primary wood, and various other types of timber would be used to achieve contrasting colors. The client had previously viewed a carving created by Triple T for a church in the Big Apple—the piece was appraised at well over one million dollars. Triple T devoted more than two years to this project's completion, delivery, and assembly. The assembly phase required more than a week, resulting in a masterpiece of art upon its completion.

Triple T is an expert at native wood carving and has also acquired the skills to carve using power tools and an occasional chainsaw. He reminisces.
"What would his grandfather say if he knew?"

This humble individual is recognized globally as the artist TTT, with his signature on each piece he produces. Furthermore, he excels in oil painting, furniture making, and other distinctive artworks.

WAR, LOVE AND FAITH

Dearest Chi,

As I sit here and listen to the war around me, I want you to know I love you more than the dry corn loves the rain. I don't know if I will ever see you again; all I know is that without you, I am lost in the dark, closed-in wilderness of the snake. I pray every day for us to be together. I miss going to bed early and getting up early. I am not used to sleeping in a sitting position, holding a rifle, and thinking of you. I'll take that back. I love thinking of you. I think about my hand feeling the warmth of your body and all the intimate moments we shared. I want my eyes to close and fall into a deep sleep, knowing you are next to me.

May an eagle and a fox rush to deliver this letter to you.

With my ever-ending love,

Triple T.

Chapter 2
Gramps' Native Philosophy.

Gramps is a full-blooded Native Indian living on land once home to the Shawnee Tribe. The love of a grandfather and grandson is never-ending. Gramps loved Tommy more than a son, and there is a special love for grandchildren.

The love of a grandfather cannot be replaced, and Gramps' love for Tommy will live on in the memories of their togetherness. Gramps was a master of wisdom, and with his wisdom, he spoke to Tommy.

He and only he would call Tommy, Tom-Tom, and whisper in Tom-Tom's ear, My Shawnee Boy, I love with the heart of the wind.

After his grandfather (Gramps) passed away, Tom-Tom would live with the memories he made with his grandfather (Gramps) throughout his life journey. To Tommy, it was a comfort to know that he had memories of the time he spent with Gramps, and now he has an eagle that looks over him.

The Shawnee Wisdom was that taking what you don't replenish from the earth was wrong.

Grandfathers are always on your side, always there to cheer you on. Grandparents are always proud of you, no matter what, and they will never stop loving you even if they disagree with your choices.

Trees and other vegetation may be cut off but never uprooted. Everything has spirits: the eagle, wolf, snake, grass, trees, rocks, etc.

The teachings imparted by Gramps will endure throughout one's lifetime. He educated TomTom in American Indian Philosophy, a discipline that provides profound insights applicable to contemporary life.

This philosophy elucidates our interactions with God's Creation on Mother Earth and underscores the importance of mutual respect among individuals.

TomTom and Gramps dedicated numerous days and nights to traversing the forest, resting by the waters, and attuning themselves to the rhythms of nature. Gramps consistently reminded TomTom:

As articulated by Tommy, concepts such as karma, destiny, fate, fortune, divine will, belief, and what many refer to as luck merit acknowledgment. However, Tommy regards these notions as integral to his spiritual beliefs; equally significant is the practice of living in accordance with them.

Profound Wisdom:

Tommy decided to compare his lessons to the lessons as they were explained in the Bible.

Lesson 1: Listen before you speak. It is imperative to listen and learn from the wisdom of those who have preceded you to advance and transform from childhood to manhood. These lessons are specifically designed to shape your character. The development of character requires, first and foremost, respect for your creator and the individuals in your vicinity. One's character should reflect an understanding of one's attitude toward essential aspects such as the creator, nourishment, water, and air; these elements are of utmost significance, as our existence relies on them. *As Tommy listened to Gramps, he absorbed all the knowledge, and perhaps that is why he succeeded in school, the Marines, and Life.*

What does the Bible have to say about: listen before you speak?

James 1:10 – Wherefore my beloved brethren, let every man be swift to hear, slow to speak, and slow to wrath." In the Bible, Proverbs has much to say about listening before speaking, and this is one that hits home.

Proverb 29-20 – "There is more hope for a fool than someone who speaks without thinking.

Lesson 2: <u>Honor</u> the Creator above and the Earth below. Acquire what you take and refrain from taking more than is necessary. Nothing is truly yours until you have earned it. Show respect for the property of others. Tommy respected nature, and if he harvested the forest, he replaced what he took.

Reference to the Bible – He discovered that the Bible teaches us to acknowledge God as the Creator and reflect His love and care for all creation. In the Bible, we are asked to protect the earth: As stewards of the earth, we are called to protect and care for it, recognizing our responsibility to maintain its integrity.

Lesson 3: <u>Rise</u> with the sun. <u>Pray</u> to the great heavens so you know to be kind to all. Make the most of the day and thank the gods as often as possible. We have much to be thankful for, so show your appreciation. *Tommy was always up before the sun, first praying to the Gods or the morning sun, and was in bed shortly after the sun went to sleep behind the mountains, thanking the Gods for a productive day. Later in life, Tommy was introduced to Jesus and began to see the similarities be-*

tween his native philosophy and Christianity.

Psalm 113:3: "From the rising of the sun to the place where it sets, the name of the Lord is to be praised."

Ephesians 4:28 – "Let the thief no longer steal, but rather let him labor, doing honest work with his own hands, so that he may have something to share with anyone in need."

Lesson 4: Respect what the earth has given us. Never mistreat a plant, animal, or person. Treat all animals, snakes, and insects as you would treat a child, not things to be killed for pleasure. These are the gifts of **_Mother Nature_** and should be treated with respect. Nature is part of us, and not something that belongs to us. It is part of our being and gives us life through air, food, and water. Never presume it belongs to you. *Tommy respected this lesson, and as he traveled, he became a master of replacing what he took. As a tree falls, it is a gift from the Gods and should become wood to build with or heat a home with. Never leave it to root. Replenish the bark and sawdust back to the earth.*

Psalm 24:1: "The earth is the Lord's, and everything in it, the world, and all who live in it." This verse clarifies that God owns the earth and all that is in it. Remember, these are gifts and should be treated with respect.

Genesis 2:15: "The Lord God took the man and put him in the Garden of Eden to work it and take care of it." This verse explains that the people/humanity are responsible for maintaining the land that has been given to us.

Lesson 5: *Put others first*, above selfish individualism or ego. Share happiness and wealth. If you have good fortune, spare a thought for those who haven't. Be charitable and kind to all, especially those who don't have as much as you do. *This is where Tommy shines; he is a master of giving.*

The Bible consistently reminds us of the importance of putting others' needs and well-being before our own. Believers should demonstrate humility and selflessness. This mindset is woven throughout scripture, urging believers to consider others more important than

themselves and to prioritize their good above all else.

Lesson 6: *Treat all children* respectfully and teach them well, for they are our future. Our children should grow to be the great minds of tomorrow. They should be treated well and respected the way an adult should treat another adult. Tommy's love for children is evident in his generosity, teaching, and affection.

The bible explains the importance of treating children with respect and kindness.

Ephesians 6:4: "Fathers, do not provoke your children to anger, but bring them up in the discipline and instruction of the Lord.

Proverbs 22:6: "Train up a child in the way he should go; even when he is old he will not depart from it."

Proverbs 29:15: "The rod and reproof give wisdom, but a child left to himself brings shame to his mother."

Lesson 7: Be Patient and Discover Your Character. This is a solo mission, so don't let others interfere with your journey. While others may be on the same path or present along the way, it is ultimately up to you to shape your future. *He never depended on others and hoped they would care for what they have and not what I have. He found numerous discrepancies, including neglected land, crumbling homes, and abandoned children. Another thing that he hated was seeing trash along the highways, and not too far away, he discovered a dump where people just threw trash (large appliances) over the hillside. Tommy soon learned the meaning of (Red Neck), and a redneck is not just the white man.*

The Bible emphasizes the importance of patience as a virtue that leads to spiritual growth and maturity.

Galatians 6:9: "Let perseverance finish its work so that you may be mature and complete, not lack anything."

Ephesians 4:2: "Be still before the Lord and wait patiently for him: fret not yourself over the one who prospers in his way."

Lesson 8: <u>Be thankful</u> for the beauty of life – Greed will kill you. When life is lived with respect, you will find beauty in all of it. *Tommy realized that his people smoked, drank, and took what belonged to others, but just because they did it did not mean it was right.*

The Bible emphasizes the importance of gratitude and thankfulness for the beauty of life. These verses encourage us to appreciate the beauty of life and to express gratitude for the blessings we have.

1 Thessalonians 5:18: Give thanks in all circumstances; for this is God's will for you in Chris Jesus."

Psalm 104:24: "How many are your works, Lord! In wisdom you made them all: the earth is full of your creatures."

Ecclesiastes 3:13: "For I know that nothing good will come out of my mouth or from my lips, but only speech and words that come from the mouth of the Lord."

Lesson 9: <u>*Be true*</u> to the wishes and words of others: To transform into a new person, allow people to speak their minds, and never try to tear them down for their thoughts. When you disagree, discuss the matter after they have finished speaking. *He would always start a heated conversation with "Please help me understand."*

The Bible teaches us to respect others' wishes and words while avoiding unnecessary criticism. It encourages us to speak the truth with love and kindness. These principles reflect God's love for humanity. The Bible also warns against being too judgmental and recommends shifting our words from criticism to encouragement, promoting a spirit of love and grace.

Matthew 7:1-3: "Do not judge, or you too will be judged. For in the same way you judge others, you will be judged, and with the measure you use, it will be measured to you. Why do you look at the speck of sawdust in your brother's eye and pay no attention to the plank in your own eye?

Tonny read a lot and knew more than most when it came to government conversation and did not believe one side was right and the other side is wrong, just like the two-party system.

Lesson 10: Don't Judge, Don't Gossip. Never talk behind someone's back: We as a nation love to gossip, but Native Americans believe that you inspire negative energy, which will only come back to you twice as hard. *He thought of a phrase, "Gossip is the news running ahead of itself, in a red satin in dress." Or "If you can't say anything nice, keep your mouth shut."*

The Bible tells us, "Let us seek to build others up, not tear them down." Most, if not everyone, has experienced the harm of gossip. God's Word warns us to stay away from people who gossip and to guard our words when speaking about others.

James 4:11: *"Brothers and sisters, do not slander one another. Anyone who speaks against a brother or sister judges them." This verse warns against speaking ill of others and emphasizes the importance of unity.*

Lesson 11: *Be forgiving:* It's important to remember that every person makes mistakes, and we must forgive quickly when someone makes an innocent or naive judgment. *His grandfather would always compliment a mistake as a learning opportunity.*

Proverbs 21:23: "Whoever keeps his mouth and his tongue keeps himself out of trouble." This verse underscores the importance of self-control in our speech.

James 4:11: "Brothers and sisters, do not slander one another. Anyone who speaks against a brother or sister judges them." This verse warns against speaking ill of others and emphasizes the importance of unity.

Lesson 12: Bad thoughts are harmful to your health. Negativity is believed to negatively affect your mental health, body, and spirit. It's essential to think positively and always strive for the right attitude. *While in Vietnam, Tommy remained positive, regardless of how difficult the situation became. He believed that is why he is alive and sane.*
Bible verses about negativity that can help combat negative thoughts and promote a positive mindset:

Matthew 6:34: "Therefore do not worry about tomorrow, for tomorrow will worry about itself. Each day has enough trouble of its own."

Proverbs 15:4: "The soothing tongue is a tree of life, but a perverse tongue crushes the spirit."

Ephesians 4:29: "Do not let any unwholesome talk come out of your mouths, but only what Id helpful for building others up."

Colossians 3:16: Let the word of Christ dwell in you richly: teach and admonish one another in all wisdom, through psalms, hymns, and songs from the Spirit, singing to God with gratitude in your hearts.

There were times, as Tommy studied the words of Jesus, that he didn't think of Gramp's and believed his grandfather would have appreciated the teaching of Christ and those of Budai.

Lesson 13: Refrain from inflicting emotional *distress upon others.* Engaging in actions that harm individuals emotionally will ultimately result in reciprocal pain for oneself. Causing unnecessary emotional suffering is unethical and will inevitably come back to the individual who perpetrates it. Strive to become more compassionate by choosing not to wound others' feelings. How did he handle emotional situations during his time in Nam?

"He would tell the soldier to sit down and write a letter of happy thoughts to someone he loved. Or he would tell him to think of everything they will do when they get home, plant that seed, and let it become you."

As time passed, Tommy began to feel the importance of helping others more deeply than ever before, both in good times and in moments of distress.

Psalm 34:18: The Lord is close to the brokenhearted and saves those who are crushed in spirit.

(Tommy thought of Mr. Cobbs, Mad-dog, No-teeth, and many others who were now living close to him, on land he felt belonged to everyone.) Matthew 5:42: "Bear one another's burdens and so fulfill the law of Christ."

As Tommy read on, he came across many verses that encouraged indi-viduals to help each other through times of distress and felt that is what Gramp's meant when he explained that the land belongs to all of us and no one man or government.

Acts 20:36: "For as in one body we have many members, and the mem-bers do not all have the same function, so we, though many, are one body in Christ."

Tommy began to think and compare his past and present, and felt so thankful that his Gramps laid a solid foundation for him to stay happy, and now through Christ, he found Chi, yet he wondered, 'Where could she be?' and with a tear or more he turned over in bed laid the Bible beside him and began to dream of Chi.

Lesson 14: ***Be honest*** and trustworthy: Never lie to save yourself. The truth will ultimately work more in your favor, even if it may hurt at the time. Act on it if you wish to transform into a new person.
This always reminded Tommy of George and Abe. George Washington's famous quote, "I cannot tell a lie, Pa; I did cut it with my hatchet." Honest Abe, they called him after he returned a penny to a customer who had been overcharged. He walked several miles to show his mis-take.

The Bible emphasizes the importance of honesty in various passages. Proverbs 12:22: "The Load detests lying lips, but he delights in people who are trustworthy."

Ephesians 4:25: "Therefore, each of you must put off falsehood and speak truthfully to your neighbor, for we are all members of one body."

Colossians 3:9: "Lie not to another, seeing that ye have put off the old man with his deeds;"

Proverbs 11:1: "A false balance is abomination to the LOAD, but a just weight is his delight."

These verses and many more value of honesty in the eyes of the LOAD and the importance of being trustworthy and truthful in all aspects of life. Honesty is always the best policy. Embracing the truth and living a life that reflects the will of the LORD.

Lesson 15: Create a healthy balance in your life: Don't overcommit yourself to every aspect of your life. Meet yourself in each area of your life. Be kind to your mental, spiritual, emotional, and physical Self, but avoid overindulgence in any one part. He would question himself about what he did to maintain his mental, spiritual, emotional, and physical well-being. Mentally, he read and studied. Spiritually, he prayed and read various philosophies, appreciating the teachings of Buddha. Emotionally, he meditated (prayed to Jesus), and physically, he ran. He was in tip-top shape, never smoked, ate healthy, and never looked at a beer as alcohol, but laughed because he lied to himself, saying it was a grain beverage.

These verses emphasize the importance of honoring Jesus through a holistic approach to our mental, physical, emotional, and spiritual well-being.

Proverbs 3:7: "Do not be wise in your own eyes; fear the LORD and shun evil. This will bring health to your body and nourishment to your bones.

Lesson 16: _Think before speaking_. It is essential to consider your thoughts before articulating them. Maintain an awareness of your cognitive processes: Consistently recognize how your thoughts may manifest in actions and assume responsibility for those actions. *He believed in listening first and speaking second. Stop speaking, and think, and listen to the thoughts of others. What does the Bible have to say about thinking before speaking? By internalizing these teachings, we can cultivate a habit of thoughtful communication that fosters understanding, empathy, and peace.*

Proverb 18:21: The tongue has the poser of life and death, and those who love it will eat its fruit."

James 1:19: Everyone should be quick to listen, slow to speak, and slow to become angry."

Proverbs 15:28: "The heart of the righteous weighs its answer, but the mouth of the wicked gushes evil."

Lesson 17: _Don't destroy what is not yours._ Respect the property of others: Never damage or touch something that doesn't belong to you without explicit permission. Invading someone's personal space is a sin. Do this if you genuinely want to learn how to become someone new. *He believed that if people practiced this, they would have very little need for prisons. The Bible presents several verses and principles of integrity and the consequences of taking what is not yours.*

Exodus 20:15: "You shall not steal."

Luke 12:33: "No thief approaches heaven."

2 Chronicles 20:15:

Lesson 18: Be yourself before anyone else: Don't let others distract you from your _true self._ If you are not true to yourself, you can't expect to be faithful to anyone else. Tommy waited for true love to come to him, and he found it in Chi. The Bible emphasizes the importance of being yourself without wearing a false face.

Philippians 2:3: "Don't act out of selfish ambition or be conceited. Instead, humbly think of others as being better than yourselves."

John 2:6: "He that saith he abideth in him ought himself also so to walk, even as he walked."

1 Corinthians 11:1: "Imitate me, as I also imitate Christ.
"Ephesians 2:10: "For we are God's handiwork, created in Christ Jesus to do good works, which God prepared in advance for us to do.

"Jeremiah 29:11: "For I know the plans I have for you," declares the Lord, "plans to prosper you and not to harm you, plans to give you hope and a future."

Lesson 19: Their choice - leave it alone. Respect others' beliefs and never try to force your own. Let people follow the religion of their choice without judgment. It's their life, and they can do what they want with it. Tommy respects all major religions and studies many, so he knows how to support his own beliefs.

The Bible teaches us to treat others with kindness, understanding, and dignity. It warns against favoritism and urges believers to treat everyone equally. The Bible also teaches us to be tolerant and understanding of those who may have different beliefs from our own. It encourages us to be open-minded and show respect for the beliefs of others, even if we don't agree with them.

Tommy had to reflect on this interpretation. He felt and thought about War and the aggressor and how many innocent people would be taken advantage of. He also thought about the bullies at school, and how they took advantage of the smaller and weaker kids, and how he would step in.

Matthew 6: "You will hear of wars and rumors of wars, but see to it that you are not alarmed. Such things must happen, but the end is still to come."

Matthew 7: "Nation will rise against nation, and kingdom against kingdom. There will be famines and earthquakes in various places.

Lesson 20: Begin an emotional conversation with – ***"Please help me understand." It seemed to work for him.***

Tommy has 21 commandments of his own. To remind him and others who would come to share bread with him, he created a large sign to hang in his workshop and numerous small wood carvings with a single statement on each plaque. These plaques are designed to remind others how to behave on their plantation. This should become a habit of living in your body and soul! The sign, read the following words and statements.

=

PRAY
Respect, Honor, Character
Early to bed, early to rise
*Take care of Mother Nature *
Put first things first
*Love and treat
*Children well *
What is your soul mission
* Be thankful*
*Be true to yourself *
Don't judge others
*Be forgiving *
Think positive thoughts
Show compassion and empathy
Be honest
Don't overcommit
Think before you speak
Don't destroy what isn't yours
Their choice – leave it alone
Love who you are becoming
Please – Help me understand

Gramps explains:

Gramps to TomTom, asking him to sit on the great rock of knowledge and listen to the beliefs passed down from many nations. We have a mountain, which is more than we need, so let the Amish use what they require, while others fish and hunt. Which is more than we need, so let the Amish use what they require, while others fish and hunt.

Remember, when the blood in your veins returns to the sea, and the earth in your bones returns to the ground, perhaps you will remember that this land does not belong to anyone; you belong to the land, so share what you have. Tommy had difficulty knowing that he put up no-trespassing signs because others did not respect the land. They would tear up the land with motor vehicles and take things that didn't belong to them. For now, he knew he had to keep the signs up and pray that the Gods and Jesus understood. "Why did he?"

One of these philosophical reminders is not more important than any other; they are all important to live by, and when you practice them, they become part of your inner spirit; they become habits. He believes these came from the Gods and Jesus. He would share these with anyone who came to live on God's land.

The old way of teaching was that tearing anything growing from its place on the earth was wrong. It may be cut off, but it should not be uprooted. The trees and grass have spirits. Whenever a good Indian destroys growth, his act is done in sadness and with a prayer for forgiveness because of his necessities. As Triple T. was battling in Vietnam, he thought. Why are we fighting over land? Why can't we all live by this Philosophy?

Triple T. could see that other men did not respect each other or the land beneath the Heavens, as the native way did before the white man invaded their nation.

They took everything from us and would take from each other so that many had less and some had more; they never learned to share the land. They forgot the Earth was their mother. This killing is not better than the simple old way of my people.

A commonsense example is that Native Americans treated the environment in the best way possible, recognizing that everyone depends on this planet. It is foolish not to take care of it, just as it is foolish not to care for our bodies.

Native American Indians believed every tree and stone was alive, and Mother Earth was a living entity deserving of respect and protection, never to be abused or misused. Caring for this planet, embracing generosity instead of greed, and respecting our brothers and sisters, combined with a worshipful lifestyle (not a Sunday-only religion), embody the soul and core of American Indian beliefs.
Ref: American Indian Philosophy - by Karlton Douglas, 2002.

Patience also came from understanding Brother Bear's lengthy hibernation. Alertness and sensitivity to their surroundings stemmed from observing the actions of Brother Deer and Rabbit. Watchfulness came from Brother Hawk's slowly, hovering, piercing gaze. Steadfast arose from the growing trees and the continuously flowing streams. Balance was evident in the changing four seasons, transitioning from hot to cold.

The planets and stars, especially the moon, moved in cycles that illustrated a continuous and balanced pattern.

The circle symbolized completeness, a prevalent figure in Native Indian Beliefs. It encompassed the American Indian beliefs that it brought balance to life. It has no beginning or end but indicates a continuum. The recurrent use of four, representing the four directions of life, formed a complete circle of life and a never-ending way of being.

Tommy T. truly values the foundation that has shaped his love and understanding of human motion, which he believes should be continuous and always evolving. He also sees the Christian cross as a beautiful reminder of salvation and a source of strength, especially when they stand together.

Tommy T. respected his Indian teachings and philosophy. He found many similarities in the teachings of Jesus, and on many Sundays, one could see him sitting in the last row of the church, absorbing every word spoken. Though he arrived late and left early, his weekly giving was generous. After church, he would go to a truck stop for lunch, questioning the minister's words and trying to find reasoning; Tommy T. would argue with himself. The words of the minister came from Psalm 1

Happy are those who do not follow the advice of the wicked or take the path that sinners travel, or sit in the seat of scoffers, but their delight is in the law of the Lord, and on his law, they meditate day and night." Phonies he thought, that is what they are; no happy faces in church, except for a few children, doing what kids do and glad to be doing it.

I see the same men at the tavern, drinking, cursing, and being extra nice to the ladies. Exodus states, *"Thou shalt not covet thy neighbor's house, thou shalt not covet thy neighbor's wife, nor anything that is thy."*

As stated, T.T.T. believes in his world and respects the teachings passed down to him from his grandfather. Yet he gets much satisfaction from the words of Jesus. He finds it simple.

"Thou Shalt and Thou Shalt Not." It all has to do with choices. My choice - Psalm 4.8 – *"In peace, I will lie down, and sleep for you alone, Lord, and make me dwell in safety."*

Tommy feels safe in his world, skills, and faith that Jesus and the Indian Gods are looking over him. It wasn't easy to find peace and sleep, but he had a way to meditate and relax in the quiet world of the spirit. He slept with one eye open.

TomTom recalls his Gramps telling him, *"When you lie down in the forest, sleep lightly, with one eye open, because the bear and the mountain lion are close by."*

In Nam, he slept lightly because it was War and his choice to be there. He never looked at the Vietnamese as the enemy. They were soldiers, just like him, and he respected their right to protect their land, but others did not. Tommy T. was a Marine, and he honored his duty. Tommy has been blessed with what is known as the second sight, which is a sense of intuition, or a silent voice from nature or Jesus letting him know he is in danger.

The war has left a heavy feeling in his heart. He often struggles to trust the orders from his higher-ups and grapples with feelings that he can't quite put into words. Even when things are uncertain and complex, he chooses not to blame others, showing a remarkable understanding.

I was a Marine who followed orders; I took an oath, code, and creed.

"I Tommy Tucker do solemnly swear that I will support and defend the Constitution of the United States against all enemies, foreign and domestic, that I will bear true faith and allegiance to the same' and that I will obey the orders of the President of the United States and the orders of their superiors.

My code:

Never lie, cheat, or steal; abide by an uncompromising code of integrity, respect human dignity, and respect others. Honor compels Marines to act responsibly, fulfill our obligations, and hold ourselves and others accountable for every action.

My creed:

Before God, I swear this creed. My rifle and I are the defenders of my country. We are the masters of our enemy. We are the saviors of my life.

He struggled with the oath he took and the code he lived by. He lay awake at night, trying not to but always questioning the conflict between his beliefs and the Bible he tried to live by.

He thought, what about Kennedy, Johnson, and Nixon – what type of moral compass were they taught to live by? And start to write a letter to Chi.

Dearest Chi,

I miss you, and my love for you keeps me moving and staying alive. Since I haven't heard from you, I will assume there is a good reason.

I continue to be smarter than I am brave – Charlie – (what we call the north) struck us today – I lost too many young men; some I knew and some just arrived. One loss hit home, a Marine I went through basic with, was killed, this pisses me off because I don't understand why we are here. My heart seems to be drawn in sorrow. The sun goes down, the sun comes up, and the wind whispers across the battlefield. As the eagle flies, I know a true warrior has fallen. The courage of a mountain lion, the strength of a bear, they fought for what they believed was right. Their spirits will continue to remind me that I am free because they, as Marines, sacrificed their lives for me. Young men just turning 20 are being taken from their families, and I ask Why. I wish there were more I could do to save lives. Last night I was able to rescue some young Marines to see them killed today.

I find myself reaching my limit with this war; my grandfather might call it a "chaa war," which loosely translates to something unpleasant. I apologize for my bluntness. That's how I see it —as SHIT WAR. I realize you might call it "chet tiet war" or just chet, and I appreciate that different terms exist. Nevertheless, the reality remains that it's still a challenging situation, no matter how we name it and to me a shit war is just a shit war.

I must stay alert so that I will sleep with one eye open and one eye closed; the eye that is shut will reflect images of you.

Forever Love

Triple T

Chapter 3
Teaching the Native Indian's way of life:

Wisdom

The Native Indians from coast to coast were Theists. A Theist is a person who believes in the existence of a god or gods, a creator who intervenes in the universe. They generally believe in a Supreme Being, a

Great Mystery, or a Great Spirit.

Triple T would say the Great Spirit is his belief and faith. His belief is as powerful to him as Jesus is to a Christian. It reflects an Indian attitude toward the Creator and helps shape Triple T's life. He believes that Mother Earth belongs to only the Creator.

He finds the teachings of Jesus to be a poignant reminder of the beauty of faith. What is interesting is that most Indian tribes have a story that is very similar to the Genesis account in the Bible. It should be noted that American Indians are often portrayed as supernatural characters labeled "bad or evil." These tribes are seen as troublemakers, and he perceives the same in American politics. The political system left a bitter taste in his mouth. His experiences in the latter part of the War left him with a lingering bitterness, akin to wormwood—bitter and non-digestible.

American Indians did not generally think of people going to Hell, but they believed that bad people would go to a bad place after they passed on, or that those bad things awaited them just before passing on. It was also believed that good people would go to the Happy Hunting Grounds, Heaven, as described in the Bible. Many Indians believed: "that their spirit would travel back to their Creator upon their death, or it would travel back to its Ancestor Land."

His grandfather taught him the Indian way of life. The Indians' general beliefs centered on their responsibility to God, His Creation, and fellow human beings. Tommy loved and appreciated the Indian Way and mused about how great the world would be if everyone thought like the peaceful Indian and less like the Evil Indian. He believed in the essence of nature and the wisdom we can apply to our everyday lives.

After serving in Vietnam, he strongly felt that, after witnessing all the unnecessary killings and bloodshed, he found much room for Indian Philosophy in his heart, believing it was up to mankind to improve the world. To him, this was essential, and we could no longer neglect the world due to greed and ignorance while ignoring the beauty of working together.

This thinking refers to the Garden of Eden, reflecting a strong and respectful approach to caring for God's great work.

Tommy T would pray to his Christian God.

"I know I'm a sinner and ask for your forgiveness. I believe Jesus Christ is your Son. I think that He died for my sin and that you raised Him to life. I want to trust Him as my Savior and follow Him as Lord, from this day forward. Guide my life and help me to do your will. I pray this in the name of Jesus. Amen."

He believed that there was a silver lining in everything. He read James 1:2-4, which says to be glad, even if you have a lot of trouble. You learn to endure by having your faith tested (and Tommy's faith was tested every day he served in Vietnam), but you must learn to endure everything to become completely mature and lacking nothing.

The nature school was conducted in the field rather than in a classroom. They taught moral and ethical respect and how to behave in every situation. The Alder tribe chiefs instilled their social wisdom. Patience was crucial; learning to be still in the moment and learn from everything experienced was vital.

"Be still and know that I am God" is a powerful verse from Psalm 45:10, emphasizing the importance of quiet contemplation and resting in God's sovereignty. Steadfastness arose with the growing trees and the continually flowing streams, much like watching a mountain lion react to a rabbit.

Students were taught to be alert and sensitive to their surroundings. They listened to the wind, smelled the air, and observed the ants and grasshoppers.

They watched their brother's deer as it fed and raised its head to listen to the wind. Watchfulness is slow, akin to a hawk hovering with a piercing eye, ready to swoop toward some trout in the stream.

They learned about balance in nature, especially by observing the four seasons. As days grew longer and shorter, they began to prepare for each season. They studied the stars, the moon, and the sun's position.

As the seasons shifted from hot to cold and back again, they realized that the four seasons combined to make a year. "Native American calendars differ from the traditional twelve-month calendars primarily used today. Though the type of calendar differed among tribes and the regions they inhabited, most Native American calendars began in the spring. This is because Native Americans placed much importance on nature and the earth, and since the spring months were when new plants and animals were born, it symbolized the beginning of a new year." *Get the Facts about the Native American Calendar (native-net.org).*

Grandfather would remind TomTom that life flows like a river. Its relentless power moves a person through several twists and turns, some good, some bad. Looking at its source to understand its unique patterns and currents is always good.

A letter from a returning veteran trying to understand the twists and turns of life.

As I recall, I was carried from the aircraft on a stretcher at Travis Air Force Base near San Francisco, California. What an unforgettable welcome; tomatoes, rotten eggs, and dog feces were thrown at me and the men in wheelchairs.

We fought for what we believed was a just cause. This war was unlike any previous wars when GIs received parades and were welcomed home as heroes.

I guess they thought we were the enemy. I was devastated, hurt, and humiliated. What the hell happened to America?

All I could see were long-haired hippie people yelling at us like it was we who started the war. All we did was enlist like any other good American.

After all, I guess Muhammad Ali was right.

Forgotten

Chapter 4
Vietnam Defending Khe Sanh. (1962)

North Vietnam (PAVN) conducted a massive artillery bombardment on the U.S. Marine garrison at Khe Sanh, situated in South Vietnam near the border with Laos. For the next 77 days, U.S. Marines and their South Vietnamese allies defended against an intense siege of the garrison, one of the longest and bloodiest battles of the Vietnam War.

The U.S. military presence at Khe Sanh began in 1962 when Army Special Forces established a small camp near the village, located about 14 miles south of the demilitarized zone (DMZ) between North and South Vietnam and 6 miles from the Laotian border on Route 9, the principal road from South Vietnam into Laos. U.S.

Marines constructed a garrison adjacent to the Army camp in 1966. In the fall of 1967, the People's Army of North Vietnam (PAVN) began to build up its strength in the region, and U.S. officials began to suspect that Khe Sanh would be the target of an attack. Khe Sanh - Location, Vietnam War & Who Won - HISTORY

Tommy thought about Lesson 3 as he served: Rise with the sun. Pray to the great heavens to remind yourself to be kind to everyone. Embrace each day and express gratitude to the gods as often as possible. There's so much to be thankful for, so let's show appreciation! But how could I share my appreciation when they want to kill me?

We rise before the sun, and I wonder if my commanding officer can pray. It can be challenging to be kind to everyone around us. As Marines, we're taught to make the most of our day. I genuinely have so much to be thankful for, especially knowing that another Marine has my back and I'm still alive. Tommy thinks of Chi and writes a letter.

Dearest Love –

I miss you daily as I try to make sense of my time here. I often feel so detached from my humanity. I can't help but see things that weigh heavily on my heart. So unprepared for battle, young men are sent to Nam, utterly unaware of the challenges they are about to face. It feels like we're being used as pawns in a complicated and harsh struggle, amidst a jungle that feels like home to the enemy.

I realize being here was my choice, and I'm reflecting on my mental well-being. Every day, I face the reality of death, and seeing young Marines, some not even 20, lose their lives profoundly impacts my sense of vitality.

The hot and humid climate of the dense jungle, combined with the challenging terrain, can be quite overwhelming for soldiers who are experiencing this environment for the first time. They face threats from diseases and wild animals, including tigers, which adds to the complexity of their situation. I used to be unfamiliar with PTSD, or Post-Traumatic Stress Disorder. Still, I now see how common it is, especially among soldiers who turn to medications or other ways to manage the stress of warfare. I've noticed a significant decline in morale, mainly due to trust issues with our commanding officers and the government. We're often treated as expendable assets in a conflict that's hard to grasp. I've seen many soldiers start to pull away from the Marines, and I understand why. It's like trying to separate a newborn from its mother and expecting the child to walk independently.

I should head back to looking after my regiment.

TTT

In early March 1971, Tommy was promoted to Master Sergeant. He agreed to undertake this role on the condition that he would be allowed to retain his position as a technical advisor. The duties are associated with the E-8 designation position, the Master Sergeant as his unit's principal Non-Commissioned Officer (NCO).

E-8 does not engage in all leadership responsibilities typically attributed to a major or lieutenant colonel; he manages equipment and programs and provides technical, tactical, and administrative support.

Tommy believed that his promotion would enable him to offer greater assistance to the troops in the field; however, it ultimately represented merely another insignia on his uniform.

Tommy advanced rapidly through the ranks; within nine years, he reached the rank of an E8 due to his bravery, intelligence, and innate ability to act appropriately in critical moments.

What are the responsibilities of a Master Sergeant? As an E-8, the Master Sergeant functions as the leading NCO of the battalion and regiment. Tommy is expected to operate independently while still adhering to commands. Although E-8s do not take on all the leadership roles of a first sergeant, they are expected to demonstrate professionalism in leadership and various duties, in which Tommy excels.

Tommy has difficulty dealing with how people are promoted and believes T. J. was passed over because of the color of his skin, which T.J. explains to Tommy, "I am used to it, that is the way it is and has been for the Negros.' No sense in crying over spilled milk, if I do dwell on it, I may get shot."

Tommy tells T.J., "I wonder what they would do if they knew I was half Native Indian." T.J. says, "They would make you their poster child." They both laugh, give a pat on the back, and move on, just like wiping up spilled milk. T.J. wants to know how Tommy managed to get through the paperwork without them noticing. Tommy explains, "I was young and had blue eyes with that hazel glow and tan skin. They just took me as an All-American football star, and on top of all that, a good-looking white boy." They laughed and got back to action.

Jesus emphasized the importance of inner transformation and repentance, encouraging people to change their minds and actions to align with God's will. He taught that a genuine change of heart leads to a new way of living and following God. Jesus' teachings also highlight the need to overcome our old ways and embrace a renewed vision in our thoughts and actions. Tommy would learn that this mindset can reveal the difference between heads and tails. Towards the end of the war, he would experience a genuine change of heart.

Dear Tommy

No one shares anything with me because I'm not your wife, but I want you to know I'm still yours and always will be. I am carrying our little one. Yes, I'm pregnant, and I'm so excited to share that it will be a boy, at least that's what I am hoping for.! I'm thinking of naming him Tommie T., after you. Or maybe Tomas T. or Theodore— honestly, I'm still deciding!

Once again, I truly hope you receive this letter. My love for you grows stronger each day, and I didn't even think that was possible! Chi

Chapter 5
Harry Cobb aka "Woody" (1982)

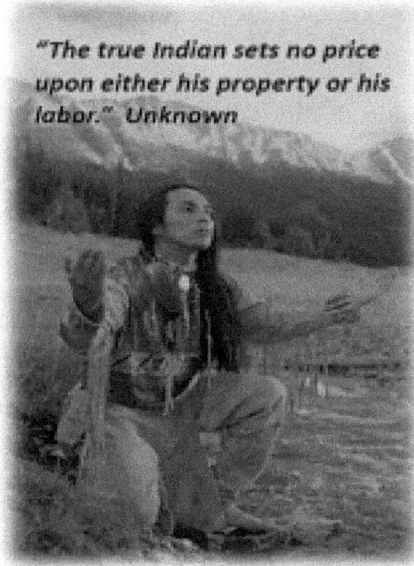

"The true Indian sets no price upon either his property or his labor." Unknown

In June of 1982, Tommy T. sat in the waiting room at the VA Hospital to see his doctor for his six-month check-up. Sitting and observing the other GIs, he thought about how blessed he was. He was particularly interested in a man who wore dirty jeans, a torn t-shirt, and had one leg. He appeared to have no worries, but looked like someone who should. The receptionist called him "Woody." Tommy wondered why his name was Woody. His real name was Harry Cobb, and he got the name Woody from his service friends because his first prosthetic looked like a pirate's wooden leg.

Tommy sat in the VA Clinic's waiting room, just listening and observing. Tommy immediately took a liking to Woody and remembered Gramps' advice. Tommy observed Woody as he was checking out. Responding to Ashley, the receptionist, *"Ashley was a charming person, always with a smile and a sense of happiness in her voice as she greeted veterans. The fantastic thing is that she knew everyone's name."* Woody said, "Yes, ma'am, no, ma'am, " smiling and tipping his hat as he turned toward the exit.

Tommy's upbringing taught him to sense when something was not right. As Woody began to walk through the parking lot, Tommy ran to his truck and caught up to Woody, rolling down the passenger's window. Tommy shouted, "Do you need a ride?"

Woody replied, "No, I'm just passing time."

He pulled his truck over, parked on the side of the road, and said,

"May I walk with you?"

Woody responded, "Why not? It is a free world."

They walked together until they came to a Dunkin' Donuts. Tommy asked Woody if he wanted a cup of coffee, and he said, "Yes, as long as it is free."

They sat down and had coffee and a donut. Before sitting down, Woody visited the restroom, and when he returned, his hair was wet, and he smelled of restroom soap.

 For about the first hour, their conversation was all about military talk and laughing, and there were moments when their eyes teared up. They talked about their injuries and a lot more.

After about an hour, Triple T. asked Woody if he needed a ride some-where, and Woody said, "No, I'm not going anywhere."

Tommy asked Woody if he would be kind enough to sit back down to have an open, honest conversation.

Woody said, "OK, what do you want to discuss?"

Tommy T. said, "You."

Harry Woody Cobb became a dear and trusted friend to T. T. Tucker. Tommy offered Woody a choice of land in the valley or on the top of his mountain, with a home.

"How can you do that, ask?" Woody asked.

TT replied, "Because I can. Tommy believes in sharing what he thinks is not his. The American Indian believed the land belonged to God.
Woody lost his leg in Afghanistan and was given a medical discharge with a pension from the Army. The GIs were overlooked during this time and had to navigate extensive government bureaucracy.

To most, this was nothing new.

During the conversation, Woody explained that he was homeless and had no family.

He returned to this area of the country because his father used to take him fishing nearby, but he had to stay in the city near the VA clinic due to a lack of transportation.

At the clinic, everyone knew Woody and treated him with respect; they understood who he was. He was simply part of the GI Family. He explained to Tommy that he felt embraced as a GI because of how people treated him. "They don't know me; they just assume I'm a drunk living on the side of the road."

Tommy T. said, "You are not homeless anymore." Woody gave him a strange look and replied, "Okay."

Tommy left Dunkin Donuts to get his reliable Ford truck, and when he got to it, he saw a ticket notice on the window and said to himself, "I should have known better."

Tommy thought of Gramps and his teachings at the Great Rock.

Lesson 5: *Put others first, above selfish individualism or ego. Share happiness and wealth. If you have good fortune, spare a thought for those who have not. Be charitable and kind to all, especially those who do not have as much as you.*

He got Woody settled into the truck. The step-up was difficult without help, and Tommy said,

"We will take care of that."

As they drove through the mountains and valleys, Woody said, "This place looks familiar." He looked at the river to his right and said, "I would love to cast a line."

Tommy T. said, "Just be patient."
Once they turned off the highway to the village,
Woody said This is where my dad took me fishing.
They drove past the church Tommy attended every Sunday, and said,
"You can go to church with me. If you want to join me this Sunday, please, please."

Woody did not like being around many people. The only place he felt comfortable was at the VA Client, because they treated him respectfully and understood his situation.

About a mile up the road, Tommy made a left, crossed over the creek, and said we could go fishing there later this week. Woody looked like a little kid in a candy store.

Woody got around well on one good leg and one missing leg. He explained that he got the name Woody at the Army Hospital in Afghanistan because his first leg looked like a pirate's wooden leg as he stood on a ship.

However, since then, Woody has had two prosthetic legs, one for walking and one for running, which he carries in his backpack, as Woody explains, "Just in case I need to run from the women after me."

Early, Woody explained that he was homeless because he was waiting for his money to be released to him from Bagram Air Base, which is the Armed Services Bank on the base. He went on to say that when he lost his leg, he was shipped back to the States before he was able to take care of any business.

Tommy said, "Not to worry; he had enough for an entire Army." And did.

Woody did not join Tommy on Sunday and would not go to the Tavern with him to eat. Woody, like many other G.I.s, suffered from Post-Traumatic Stress Disorder, better known as PTSD. He experienced flashbacks, and Tommy understood the yelling as Woody suddenly jumped from his bed to the floor, standing in a cold sweat and balancing on one good leg.

Tommy asks Woody if he is up for a shopping trip to get a step-up for the truck and some new clothes. Woody only had a backpack with everything he owned: his second leg, the army knife he could flip to hit a rabbit from twenty feet away, a few T-shirts, and army jeans. The most important possession was his dog tags- one that he wore and one that he kept in his shoes, just in case something happened, so the military could identify him. G.I.s who return with two tags are always thankful it was not their time.

Just after the sun went down, and Woody settled in, he could hear a harmonica whistling through the valley. It was pleasant to listen to the sounds of the valley and focus on the moment's beauty. He truly enjoyed the sound of a train rumbling over the tracks and the smell of clean sheets.

A visit to the city and shopping, which both gentlemen regarded with disdain. Woody procured all the required items, ranging from jeans to toothpaste and a pair of boots- one suitable for wear and the other intended for conversion into a flowerpot. To clarify, he could comfortably wear a pair of shoes due to his prosthetic limb. Furthermore, he acquired an exceptional winter parka of military caliber, along with gloves and a hat. Tommy graciously settled the bill, which totaled $

When Tommy offered Woody a parcel of land for construction, Woody responded, "I appreciate your generosity, but why do you want to do this?"

Tommy endeavored to elucidate the wisdom inherent in his tribe, which was rooted in the Native American philosophy of his grandfather, teachings he acquired from his parents.

Tommy's father was a full-blooded Shawnee, and his mother was a full-blooded Serbian American, who he believed also had German ancestry. Limited in his recollections of his parents, Tommy relies on his grandfather to provide essential information regarding their lives. He is aware that they resided and were employed in proximity to the VA Hospital and that they tragically lost their lives in an automobile accident. However, he possesses scant details surrounding these events.

Some of the information he gathered concerning his parents' lives came from rumors shared by the Amish community and peers from his educational experiences.

Tommy was not inclined towards small talk and struggled to form friendships; he was acutely aware of the negative sentiments directed towards him due to his mixed heritage as a half-Indian. Consequently, he embraced a solitary existence, like Woody, believing they would cultivate a profound relationship.

Woody indicated that we share a common experience.

"I also lost my parents in a car accident, just before being deployed to Afghanistan, shortly after graduating from high school."

When Tommy presented his workshop to Woody, he was unaware that Woody was also a woodcarver and possessed expertise in furniture-making.

Woody utilized his utility knife for carving, which constituted his sole tool. He disclosed that he had abstained from using power tools since high school and two years of trade school. Woody received national honors for his craftsmanship while in trade school, where he was acknowledged as one of the top students in the nation for unique furniture design.

They continued their journey up the gentle hill to allow Tommy to demonstrate to Woody a parcel of land offering a magnificent view of the lake, which would serve as an excellent location for construction. A makeshift road suitable for four-wheelers existed. Upon reaching the summit, Woody observed an open field encircled by evergreens, presenting a vista that would captivate those who appreciate God's creation and cherish the simple beauty of nature.

Woody recognized this as integral to his dream, a place where he could experience solitude.

Tommy remarked, "It is my gift to you because the gods told me to." Furthermore, he explained to Woody that there were plenty of vehicles for him, including four-wheelers and snowmobiles.

Woody began comprehending Tommy's character, his inherent goodness and moral convictions. As they walked along, Tommy would stop and lie prone on the ground to engage more intimately with the scent of the land.

He explained to Woody that the land can communicate, contingent upon one's willingness to listen.

A foul odor indicates that the land is degraded and unsuitable for cultivation, yet it remains advantageous for hunting.

Conversely, a sweet fragrance signifies that the location is optimal for planting.

Woody asked Tommy, "What does the soil convey to you?" Tommy replied, "This land is your home." They exchanged glances and smiled, as fate intended—a subtle smile accompanied by a nod of acknowledgment.

Dear Chi, July 1982

My dearest love. Today marks five years since I came home, and the gods- or was it Jesus? - spoke to me. They told me to help a friend, and I will because I can. Whenever we can, we should help others. I beg the gods every moment of every day to send you to me. My heart is strong, but not happy. You are my happiness, and as I write this letter, knowing it will never reach you, I have comfort in my heart as I think about you.

Until then, Love TTT

Chapter 6
Building a Home for Woody:

Tommy visited his friends Luke and Jacob, who owned a farm on the opposite side of the mountain near the lake.

Woody's plot depicts their village. Tommy introduces Woody to Luke and Jacob and proceeds to explain Woody's circumstances.

Jacob, a skilled lumberjack, consistently identifies specific trees suitable for carving. Although these trees are situated on Tommy's property, he was willing to compensate Jacob generously, as he valued quality and believed in fair payment.

However, Jacob responded, "Give me a week, and I will see what we can do for our neighbors."

Many years have elapsed since Tommy's grandfather granted Luke and Jacob's grandfather forty acres and a mule to assist their families in establishing themselves in America.

Numerous Amish families from Germany settled in the gently rolling hills across the valley from Tommy's hilltop, and he was acquainted with many of them and their families.

Tommy felt more comfortable in the presence of the Amish because their customs were closely aligned with those of the American Indians. General Theodore Tomas Tucker, a wealthy landowner, once owned this land.

The land was sold to the General by the government for fifty dollars upon his discharge. Never married, no children, but always native women to keep him warm.

After he died in the late 1800s, Tommy's great-grandfather inherited the land, which was eventually handed down to Gramps with more money than anyone would ever need. So the story goes.

In a week, the Amish community built a home for Woody: free labor, lumber, and a title cleared at the county courthouse. The house included a beautiful kitchen, a living room, three bedrooms, and two bathrooms. This marked a new beginning for Woody, one for which he would always be grateful.

Over the years, Tommy and Woody became the best of friends. Woody attends church with Tommy but is reluctant to visit the Tavern. The church offered a place where Tommy and Woody could leave before the conversation began.

However, to Woody, the Tavern would be filled with many talkative people and hundreds of staring eyes, which was not the same as the church, where they sat in the back and could leave if it became too uncomfortable. All Woodt required was a handshake built on faith.

Tommy and Woody collaborated to create all the furniture for Woody's new residence. Woody demonstrated an aptitude for learning and quickly commenced crafting furniture independently, gaining recognition for his distinctive designs. He produced items that commanded prices in the thousands of dollars, in addition to his woodcarvings. Tommy and Woody were skilled craftsmen; Tommy was developing a wall installation for an office building in downtown Manhattan, which was anticipated to fetch well over five hundred thousand dollars. Meanwhile, Woody persisted in carving small pieces and acquiring proficiency in chainsaw sculpting. His heart-shaped sculpture, carved from a solid block of wood, garnered popularity, as did his representations of bears, eagles, and birds. Notably, his eagle carvings sold for more than a thousand dollars.

Woodworking began filling the workshop, and Tommy had the great idea of searching for a storefront in New York City. Your craftsmanship is truly one-of-a-kind and deserves to be shared with the public! What do you think? Tommy asked. I'm not so sure about living among so many people. Tommy reassured, "You won't have to! We can find someone to run the gallery for us."

The Art Gallery will highlight both our primitive and modern works of art! While moving to the Big Apple can come with its challenges,

After much brainstorming, they decided against New York City and would try an alternative plan. They decided to stay close to home and purchased a great piece of land, not far from their workshop.

The land was on a bustling highway connecting two major highways, which was a plus.

Like in the movie The Field of Dreams, they decided to build it, knowing that "THEY WILL COME. "

My dearest Love, Chi,

I don't recall mentioning my Friend Woody. Long story as to why he is called Woody, something to do with a wooden leg. He is now a resident of the valley. He and I are building an enterprise to serve the world in wooden crafts and furniture. I look forward to your meeting him; he is a remarkable man.

Until I hold you in my arms.
Triple T.

Chapter 7
Chi Le, born 1950:

Tommy referred to her as Chi. He met her in Saigon at a BBQ, which was more like a bar and grill. Many GIs frequently visited it seeking drinks, dancing, and entertainment. Better known as Char Stu in Cantonese, it was delicious, moist pork grilled to perfection and slightly coated with a sweet and tangy BBQ sauce.

Chi Le was a warm-hearted and genuinely innocent soul. From the first moment she saw Tommy, she felt a spark of love, although he seemed utterly unaware of her presence. Two somewhat shy or reserved individuals may have difficulty or the courage to converse.

While working as a waitress at Dim Tu Tac, a cozy spot welcoming American GIs, Chi often saw Tommy enjoying a beer at the bar with a side of pork. Little did she know, Tommy had noticed her; she was the main reason he frequented the restaurant.

At 18 - 1968 years old, Chi lived independently in a Catholic Home nearby. This welcoming Catholic Home supported young ladies who had graduated from the orphanage at age 16. She always cherished her Sundays, dedicating that time for reflection and devotion. The modest church at the home was the only Christian church in the area.

The home housed many young ladies. Speaking many languages was a plus for Chi because she could learn many other languages; it came naturally to her. It was either because of the right side or the left side of her brain. She was constantly reminded that her brain did not work like other people's brains. "Your brain is not normal."

Chi's parents were tragically killed by soldiers from the North when she was ten years old, leading her to navigate life autonomously since that pivotal moment. At a young age, Chi left the north and found refuge in the south at the orphanage for girls.

Never meeting Chi before this moment, sister Mary acted as if she knew everything about Chi Le. With her parents' teachings, Chi was no stranger to Jesus Christ. Chi believes Christ found her long before she found him.

Fortunately, she located the Christian orphanage just outside of Saigon. Traveling, which felt like a lifetime trying to avoid major roads, troops, and villages, she traveled through the rice fields and jungle of the south. The orphanage was affiliated with the Catholic Church, which Chi's father financially supported. The orphanage would provide her with refuge from the streets.

At the orphanage, she received three meals a day and a clean room with sheets that she was responsible for washing, drying, and ironing. She attended the Academy, which was the best learning school in Vietnam. School and learning more about Jesus were what she enjoyed most. School was conducted all year, with no breaks except for Christmas. Chi was exceptional when it came to learning and caring for herself. She was an honor student at the school. She appeared to be years beyond many of her classmates.

At home, she was treated like a princess; however, she was responsible for many essential living needs, such as doing her laundry and ironing, even though there were servants to care for her. She may have been dressed in the finest lines, but she also greatly respected those who had less; she was raised that way.

In 1962, Chi was 12 and lived in Ben Tre in the Mekong Delta close to Saigon. Her father was an affluent businessman in the North. He specialized in expensive jewelry and imports from China, diamonds from Africa, and gold and silver where he could find it.

Chi and her mother would travel with him on business trips whenever possible. Chi loved language and began speaking many of the foreign languages that she heard. She was a frequent visitor to the city library, where she would read all the classics.

Chi and Sister Mary would sit for hours discussing the writings of great writers, such as Ernest Hemingway and F. Scott Fitzgerald. They are known for their realistic writings. Fitzgerald is known for his realistic portrayals of the Jazz Age and the "Lost Generation. Chi believes his writing style was more descriptive than that of Hemingway, and Sister Mary speaks of him always searching for meaning within the social class. Like in "The Great Gatsby," He focused on how the characters live for wealth and status to mask deeper feelings of emptiness and loss.

Chi responds that Gatsby wanted to win back Daisy and felt his pursuit of wealth would be the answer. She explained that he would have lavish parties to cope with his emotional void left by war. She felt this disillusionment portrayed the American Dream.

Sister Mary agrees and adds that she believes they were disconnected from reality regardless of their lavish lifestyle.

Sister Mary soon realized that Chi is a profound thinker. She should not struggle with her lessons; perhaps she is more advanced in some areas than the professor.

The lost generation was a term that embraced the writers of post-World War II, such as Ernest Hemingway, known for "The Sun Also Rises, A Farewell to Arms, For Whom the Bell Tolls, and The Old Man and the Sea."

Scott Fitzgerald, best known for The Great Gatsby, and others, all of whom Chi and Sister Mary read.

Chi takes a moment to reflect as the light from the flames begins to illuminate the sky behind her. As the black smoke gently rises toward the heavens, she feels the weight of knowing that her parents, home, and all

her cherished books are lost forever.
She asks God, "Please let me live."

Chi's family wealth opened the doors to an excellent education. Her parents supported the South's political platform, appreciating its approach to government freedom.

Before the conflict, the North was called "Viet Minh," a communist national group dedicated to gaining independence from French colonial rule in northern Vietnam.

They were seen as supporters but soon faced invasion by Northern supporters for their financial backing of the southern government.

In the southern region of Vietnam, the VC, or Viet Cong, emerged as courageous guerrilla fighters.

It's essential to recognize that the government's rule in the South wasn't widely welcomed and encountered increasing opposition. The Viet Cong and the National Liberation Front played a vital role as key fighters against Diem during those early stages of the conflict.

As their home was being raided and torn apart, Chi's father managed to lift her from a back window to the ground. He tossed her his wallet and gold watch, gently saying,

"I love you, run to the church, see sister Mary."

As she ran, her heart beating with the fear that she might never see her parents again, she couldn't help but keep looking back. She watched in despair as her parents were... shot and beheaded in front of their beautiful home, an experience she would never be able to erase from her mind. Everything turned black, except for a path that seemed to appear from the heavens. She thought her parents must be in heaven, showing her the way, or was it just Jesus? She did know, but she ran like a deer being hunted by a man on a cold night in the fall.

Chi meets Tommy:

Woo Tee, the friendly barmaid, offers Tommy heartfelt advice on formally meeting Chi. Advice to Tommy from Woo: " Go to church at the orphanage; she is there every Sunday.

" Chi Le would return to the orphanage every Sunday to attend the chapel, and it was there that she finally met Tommy. Just outside the church, Chi finally encounters Tommy, eagerly awaiting a glimpse of her as she walks toward the entrance.

As their eyes meet, Tommy takes a casual step forward and greets her. "Are you the waitress from...?" (like he didn't know) he asks, prompting Chi Le to respond with a quick "Yes," before he could even finish his thought.

Their eyes locked, and an invisible force drew them closer.

Tommy and Chi nervously make their way into the cozy little chapel. With its simple cross at the altar and inviting benches, the chapel feels like a welcoming space.

Although Tommy remains unsure about Christianity, his curiosity about Jesus leads him to know that Chi is there every Sunday, and he wants to learn more.

On a specific Saturday, Tommy encountered Chi while delivering Christmas toys for children. He had carved numerous items for the children at the orphanage, consistently carrying a block of wood with an army knife. Whether on the base or at battle, he was often observed carving during his leisure time.

On this particular Saturday, Chi was helping to get ready for the children's annual Christmas party. One might ponder how Chi became aware of the toy delivery that Saturday, or whether Tommy was cognizant of her presence.

Sister Mary introduced Chi to Tommy. Both individuals comported themselves as though they had never met before this occasion.

After church, Tommy walked out with Chi Le and said, "Can I see you again?"

Chi Le replied, "Yes, you can see me waiting tables at Dim Tu Tac or here at the Chapel, I am here every Sunday."

After their fifth meeting, Tommy attended church (chapel) every Sunday when he could. He was allowed to walk Chi Le home, but was not invited in. Chi Le held her Christian values dear to her heart and knew that if she invited Tommy in, she would break those commandments.

There were Sundays when Tommy could not attend church because of Marien's duty. However, Chi Le was always there, hoping to see him.

After about a year, there came that special Sunday when Chi Le warmly invited Tommy into her living quarters at the Christian home, marking a moment when those commandments were gently broken.

Shortly after the war intensified, Tommy received his call to the front lines.

Tommy asked Chi Le to marry him, and she said yes. They set a date, and Tommy began to plan to leave the Marines and return to America with Chi Le.

However, none of this happened. The war intensified, and Tommy was in battle for longer and longer periods. Chi Le began planning to move to Canada, where she would hopefully be safe.

Chapter 8

The History of the War and How We Got There.

Understanding the war and how the events kept Tommy and Chi Le apart is essential. Tommy and other GIs dedicated their hearts and souls to the red, white, and blue. They fought in numerous battles, in the rice fields and jungle, the rice fields were muddy, hot and one had to continuously look for land mines, The jungle was hot, and downright miserable, you had to cut your way through with their machete. This was as close to hell as one could get. Tommy was considered an expert on war strategies. He was also called upon as an advisor to the Commanding Officer and participated in various Strategic Meetings.

In December 1960, the National Liberation Front, commonly known as the Viet Cong, emerged to challenge the South Vietnamese government. A civil war erupted over control of South Vietnam, as Hanoi sought to unite the country under its communist leadership.

In the spring of 1961, the administration of John F. Kennedy expanded U.S. support for the South Vietnamese government.

In August 1964, the U.S. government received word that two North Vietnamese torpedo boats had attacked U.S. destroyers in the Gulf of Tonkin.

President Lyndon Johnson requested authorization from Congress for military force, resulting in the Gulf of Tonkin resolution, which laid the groundwork for the full-scale U.S. military commitment to Vietnam.

In 1965, President Johnson dramatically escalated U.S. involvement in the war. He authorized a series of bombing campaigns, most notably Operation Rolling Thunder, and committed hundreds of thousands of U.S. ground troops to the fight.

The 1968 Tet Offensive, a bold North Vietnamese attack on the south, convinced many U.S. officials that the war could not be won at a reasonable cost.

Richard Nixon campaigned for the presidency with a "secret plan" to end the war in Vietnam. Once in office, his administration sought "peace with honor." Nixon ultimately expanded the war into neighboring Laos and Cambodia while simultaneously encouraging the "Vietnamization" of the war effort, which entailed the gradual withdrawal of U.S. troops and an increasing reliance on the South Vietnamese armed forces.

By the end of 1969, the number of American troops in Vietnam had been cut in half.

The Paris Peace Accords established the terms under which the last remaining U.S. troops in Vietnam would be withdrawn.

In 1975, the North Vietnamese finally achieved their objective of uniting the country under one communist government.

The Socialist Republic of Vietnam was formally established on July 2, 1976, and Saigon was renamed Ho Chi Minh City.

The war in Vietnam had lasting consequences for U.S. foreign policy. Congress passed the War Powers Act in 1973 in an apparent attempt to reassert control over foreign policymaking and impose constraints on presidential power.

For well over a decade, American public opinion was hostile to the idea of foreign interventions. This was known as the "Vietnam syndrome," which involved an unwillingness to become bogged down in foreign wars where American national security interests were unclear.

WAR, LOVE AND FAITH

The War: The Vietnam War started due to the United States' strategy of "containment," aimed at minimizing the spread of communism worldwide during the Cold War.

Vietnam was temporarily divided into the North Communist and the South anti-communist after the signing of the Geneva Treaty in 1954, which ended the French colony.

The French lost control of Vietnam toward the end of the Korean War. The U.S. feared that Vietnam would also fall under the power of the Communists, who intervened to prevent South Vietnam from falling.

Their intervention sparked several battles collectively referred to as the Vietnam War.

1.Battle of Ia Drang - November 14 to 18, 1965, in the La Drang Valley, South Vietnam. The Battle of Ia Drang is the first significant engagement between the U.S. Army and the People's Army.

2.Tommy was wondered during this battle and spent two weeks in the hospital and demanded he be returned to the battlefield. He was shot in the shoulder.

3. The Battle of Khe Sanh occurred in South Vietnam, in the province of Quang Tri, from January 21, 1968, to April 9, 1968.

Tommy fought in this battle and thought he would be able to return to Chi, but in the military things always change, and especially during battle.

4.Tet Offensive - The Tet Offensive was a significant military campaign during the Vietnam War, launched on January 30, 1968, by North Vietnam and the Viet Cong, a distinct political organization, against South Vietnam and its American allies. This offensive became one of the most pivotal military operations of the Vietnam War and marked a key turning point.

As the North Vietnamese and the Viet Cong failed to achieve a military victory and people at home began to look at the war differently, Public opinion and our involvement began to swing negatively. The shift in public perception added pressure on the Johnson administration, which ultimately led to a change in U.S. policy and the eventual withdrawal of troops.

5. Battle of Hue - The Battle of Hue was among the bloodiest and longest battles fought during the Vietnam War. During this battle, the forces of the U.S. Army, ARVN, and the U.S. Marine Corps engaged and defeated the PAVN and the Viet Cong.

Over the following month, from January 31 to February 28, 1968, the PAVN and Viet Cong armies were driven out after intense fighting, with the Allies declaring victory. Nonetheless, the city of Hue suffered extensive destruction, resulting in the deaths of 5,000 civilians.

Sgt. Tucker knew he was at battle but was having a difficult time understanding what was going on; he found himself questioning his commander, who was constantly changing the plan, and he heard the sound of a bomb and days later woke up in a military hospital. He had no way of contacting Chi, and at this point he didn't know where he was nor did he know where she was. He just knew he was hit with shrapnel and was covered with bandages.

He knew he led his troops through numerous battles, sustaining wounds but always finding his way back to the front line. Some thought he had a death wish, but after meeting Chi he had a reason to return. He ask the nurse, "where am I." and she said, "You are in the hospital." "But where?" The nurses Jeanne and Ema, continued to answer his questions. Jeanne responds, you were dropped of by "Huey" helicopter, and we have no way of knowing where you came from." Nurse Ema added, It is part of Operation Rolling Thunder, Let us be happy you are alive. Tommy responds, "but I have to get back to my troops.

6. Operation Rolling Thunder - Operation Rolling Thunder was a sustained aerial campaign conducted by the 2nd Air Division of the U.S. Navy and the South Vietnamese Air Force (VNAF) against the North Vietnamese from March to November 1968.

7. Battle of Hamburger Hill—The Battle of Hamburger Hill lasted eleven days, from May 10 to May 20 in 1969, between the ARVN (Army of the Republic of Vietnam) and U.S.

Army forces against the PAVN (People's Army of Vietnam). This engagement occurred on Hill 937, nicknamed Hamburger Hill due to its grueling nature.

8. Easter Offensive of 1972 - The Easter Offensive was conducted the PAVN against ARVN and U.S. troops from March to October 1972.

The north suffered significant loses nearly 100,000 casualties. The south with American air support managed to halt the north, but also had some 10,000 killed and many more wounded.

The unsuccessful Operation Lam Son.

This was his limit and he was at the point of no return; it seemed like nothing was working, communications were breaking down, and he was not receiving enough support. Many felt the USA administration didn't care, and he was beginning to believe that our leadership didn't care. The objective was to disrupt the Ho Chi Minh Trail in Laos, and we failed to achieve our objective. This resulted in heavy losses and forced withdrawal. He recalls asking for air support from the south, and time after time, he was getting zero response. He continued to ask for air support and was surrounded by troops from the north. He continued to yell, we need help, and if we don't get help, we are to lose all that we fought for.

He recalls hearing, we have unfavorable conditions. The weather is keeping us grounded. There were leadership issues that were questionable. It is not that the helicopter pilots did not want to fly, it was all about a general not wanting to pit his ass on the line. The north seemed to be better prepared than the military of the south.

Afterwards, the morale of the South and the US Marines suffered. The NVA was well-prepared and fiercely turned south back. Furthermore, international political considerations added to the frustrations. The operation failed to achieve its strategic goal. The losses were heavy all of 8,000 SVA killed and 1,462 US casualties, according to LibGuides.

Some 100 helicopters and 150 tanks were lost.

Tommy wonders how I survived.

9. Operations Linebacker I & II - Operations Linebacker I & II were U.S. Air Force and Navy campaigns against the North Vietnamese during the later phases of U.S. involvement in the Vietnam War. Operation Linebacker I occurred from May to October 1972, while Operation Linebacker II took place from December 18 to 29, 1972.

10. Battle of Xuân Lộc – LOC – meaning "bud" was a symbol meaning growth, promise, and potential. It also meant to shine bright. The Battle of Xuân was the last major confrontation of the Vietnam War. It occurred from April 9 to April 20, 1975, in and around Xuân. This battle represented the final attempt by ARVN (Army of the Republic of Vietnam) to halt the advance of PAVN (People's Army of Vietnam) and US troops and South Vietnam after its significant defeat in the city of Hue.

Due to the town's isolation, the ARVN troops were compelled to withdraw from the battle line. The Battle of Xuân dealt a significant blow to the ARVN (Army of the Republic of South Vietnam) and South Vietnam's leadership, leading to President Thieu's resignation. The pathway to Saigon was ultimately opened for the PAVN forces.

11. Fall of Saigon – The victory at Xuân paved the way for the PAVN forces to capture Saigon, the capital of South Vietnam.

12. By April 27, 1975, over 100,000 PAVN troops had surrounded the city, while only 60,000 ARVN troops remained to defend it.

However, many ARVN troops joined civilians fleeing the city. The fall of Saigon was completed with the evacuation of U.S. forces, culminating in the end of the Vietnam War on April 30, 1975, which led to Vietnam's reunification and an increase in communism throughout the country.

Why Did the Vietnam War Start? The Vietnam War, also known as the Second Indochina War, was fought in Vietnam, Laos, and Cambodia between North and South Vietnam. The North received support from China and the Soviet Union, while the United States, Thailand, Australia, and South Korea backed the South.

The National Liberation Front, also called the Viet Cong, was a South Vietnamese armed resistance group that assisted the North Vietnamese

Army (NVA). The resistance and the NVA fought to unify the country, while the South aimed to establish independence from the North.

Today, the Vietnamese people refer to the war as the Resistance War Against America. Unlike many other wars, the Vietnam War did not have a formal declaration.

However, it is widely accepted that the war began on November 1, 1955, and ended on April 30, 1975.

The U.S. involvement in Vietnam started as early as 1950 when Harry Truman sent military advisors to assist the French. However, direct U.S. military action in Vietnam began in 1964 and continued until 1973.

Causes Of the Vietnam War

Since the 19th century, Vietnam has been under colonial rule. During the Second World War, Japan invaded the country. Vietnamese political leader Ho Chi Minh, inspired by Chinese and Soviet communism, formed the League for the Independence of Vietnam (Viet Minh) to drive out both the Japanese invaders and the French colonialists.

After the United States forced Japan to surrender during the Second World War, it withdrew its troops from Vietnam, leaving Emperor Bao Dai in power.

Ho Chi Minh saw an opportunity to seize control and immediately rose in arms. He took control of Hanoi and declared the Democratic Republic of Vietnam (DRV), naming himself the president. Backed by the French, Emperor Bao established the state of Vietnam in July 1949, choosing Saigon as the capital city.

Although both parties desired a united country, Ho and his supporter's favored communism, while Bao and many others wanted to create a nation based on Western culture. The ideological difference led to one of the world's longest and most brutal wars.

The North won the battle at Dien Bien Phu in May 1954, ending French rule in the South. In July 1954, a treaty was reached to split the country along the 17th parallel. However, the treaty also called for an election two years later to unify the country. A year later, anti-communist leader Ngo Dinh Diem ousted Emperor Bao from power and became the president of South Vietnam.

Domino Theory

In 1961, President John F. Kennedy sent a team of experts to report on the conditions in South Vietnam. The team advised the president to increase the presence of American soldiers and provide technical and economic aid to assist the South in combating the Viet Cong resistance. Kennedy believed that if communism thrived in one Southeast Asian country, the rest would be compromised, and communism would spread uncontrollably.

Consequently, Kennedy increased economic aid to South Vietnam and deployed thousands of U.S. troops. By 1962, about 9,000 American troops were stationed in the country, a significant increase from only 800 in the 1950s. *Ref: www, World Atlas*

Why Did the Vietnam War Start? –

Master Sergeant Tommy T. Tucker fought many battles in Vietnam and began to lose the meaning of why they were there. More than 3 million people (including over 58,000 Americans) were killed in the Vietnam War, and more than half of the dead were Vietnamese civilians. He had no answer to Why?

Tommy wants to know if Chi Le was one of those civilians. He missed her tender and innocent smile, beauty, and companionship; he knew she was his everlasting love. He understood the War had brought them together, but it ultimately tore them apart, and he became bitter.

Not knowing where Tommy was, Chi Le was forced to leave the city in April 1975, but she knew he would be her first and only love. The last time she saw Tommy was in January 1972. Tommy said, "We will marry as soon as I return." Unfortunately, Tommy never returned due to the tumultuous events occurring in Vietnam that led to his being taken from the city to fight in various battles. Tommy deeply loved Chi Le and could not wait to return to Ho Chi Minh and marry her.

When he finally returned in June 1975, the war was over, but Chi Le was nowhere to be found.

Former CBS News correspondent Ed Bradley filed a report that many at home would see on the "CBS Evening News" on April 30, 1975. Bradley's reporting focused on the evacuation that was unfolding as North Vietnamese forces—the South's enemy, and America's—closed in on Saigon. Chi Le was among the crowd. She was taken by helicopter to a ship and was shipped off to Guam. In response to the emergency, the U.S. military established a refugee camp on this small island in the Pacific.

In Guam, the U.S. government planned to assess the crisis and process individuals while preparing camps on the mainland for the incoming Vietnamese. However, approximately 1,500 Vietnamese had another idea—refusing resettlement in the U.S. and returning home. Chi Le was one of them, hoping she would return and find Tommy.

In late 1976, Chi Le returned to Ho Chi Minh City, which was nothing like it had been when she left. She had a difficult time finding work and refused to become a prostitute, which was the main occupation for women.

Chi Le found work on a farm in the Mekong Delta, about three hours away by train or a two-day walk, but it took her three days to get there. Mostly, women worked on farms, and they provided housing. Chi Le was able to find work through her Christian church. She was treated with respect and lived in a Christian community that helped care for

Tommy Le. Tommy Le was around three when they went to the Mekong Delta. Chi Le dreamed of returning to Ho Chi Minh City and finding Tommy T. Little Tommy Le was born on April 15, 1973.

Tommy T. never knew that Chi Le was with a child. Tommy Le was a Vietnamese refugee born in Guam at Camp New Life. At the age of 35, Mr. Tommy T. Tucker became a father, and at the age of 26, Chi Le became a mother.

Tommy spent over a month in Saigon looking for Chi Le; he even went to the church that helped her get a job, but Chi Le was still in Guam then. They explained to Tommy that she could have been among the thousands who were killed. When Chi Le returned to Saigon and asked about Tommy, she heard he was looking for her. She was thankful he was still alive. They explained to her that Tommy was heading back to the States and perhaps assumed she had been killed during the war.

Opposition to the war in the United States bitterly divided Americans, even after President Richard Nixon signed the Paris Peace Accords and ordered the withdrawal of U.S. forces in 1973. Communist forces ended the war by seizing control of South Vietnam in 1975, and the country was unified as the Socialist Republic of Vietnam the following year.

Before Tommy left for the Front Line, he explained to Chi Le that he wanted to marry her and take her home with him, but did not know where home would be.

Little did Chi know she was expecting their son. Tommy found a quaint apartment in the city for him and Chi to share. In between battles, Tommy would visit. His final visit was in or around June.

Chapter 9
Baby Tommy Le and his mother's Love

According to popular belief, God cannot be present everywhere, so He created mothers. The bond between a mother and her son is always unconditional. Only one woman can love a man more than she loves herself.

Of all the types of love, a mother's is the strongest. The love between mother and child arises instantly, as a bond uniting two bodies and souls. A mother's love is unconditional and eternal.

When we say that nature is wise, we refer to the bond between a mother and her children. A mother's instinct to protect her offspring begins from the moment she knows she is pregnant.

Over the following nine months, although she has yet to see her child, he or she becomes the most precious thing in the world. Her unborn child becomes her motivation on her journey to the Mekong Delta, where she will find refuge and peace of mind.

If every person experienced love as Chi Le did for Tommy T., there wouldn't be enough land to contain that affection. Chi Le realized that with Tommy T., she felt both safe and joyful.

He shielded her from danger and enveloped her in love. Chi Le recognized that she would no longer need to seek genuine love because she had discovered it with Tommy. She felt it permeated her emotions, like a spirit entering her soul, and she knew that life without Tommy was unimaginable; she could envision herself with no one else.

She sensed the honeymoon phase had ended, and with the child she was carrying, her connection to him was eternal. Tommy Le would represent their bond, even if she never saw him again. Chi Le was sure she had a son.

While lying in the bed she had once shared with Tommy T, she whispered to him, "We'll be okay," her hand resting on her growing belly, where she felt the tiny heartbeat. "We'll be okay." A smile crossed her face as she pictured his little face and hands, imagining the smile that would brighten her life. A healthy kick reminded her of strong legs and waving arms running along the shore, accompanied by laughter—there would be laughter.

She briefly thought of Tommy's beautiful blue eyes, smile, strong hands, and square shoulders; she couldn't imagine him not being part of her life. If he were dead, how would she tell her son about the man who was his father? How would he ever know his deep compassion for those in need, his love for children, and the joy he brought them with the toys he carved?

As she lay in bed, she thought about how it would be without him.

"I'll just love him more," Chi Le asserted as she lifted herself from the bed, slightly unsteady with her altered center of gravity.

Chi Le caught her reflection in the small mirror Tommy had given her. She smiled at her reflection and giggled.

"You are having a baby!" Undaunted by the hard road ahead, Chi Le reached for her work clothes, wiggled into the ever-tightening jumpsuit, and noticed how it was covered with rice and dirt stained from days in the rice paddies. She smiled and simply said.

"I'm having a baby, and we will be okay." That thought reminisced in her thoughts throughout the day, week, etc.

Dear Tommy

I hope you know how much I love you. My thoughts and prayers are with you twenty-four hours a day. Awake, you are there, I work, you are there, I lie down to sleep, and this is when you are there. I don't believe I can ever forget the love I have for you. You are the kindest, most caring man I have ever met. Praying to see you standing beside our bed when I open my eyes.

Love Chi

Chapter 10
Where is Chi Le?

Tommy sat quietly on his front porch, staring at the stars as he thought about Chi Le. He asked Jesus, "Is she okay? Where is she? Is she alive? Please let me know."

At that moment, a shooting star streaked across the sky, sending a wave of warmth through Tommy, assuring him that Chi Le was alive. He jumped off the porch, raced down the road, and up the hill to Woody's, yelling, "She's alive! Woody, she's alive!"

Standing on his porch, Woody looked at Tommy and said, "Who is alive?"

Tommy answered, "Chi Le, the woman I love." Inquisitively, Woody asked, "How do you know?"

Tommy replied, "Jesus told me." Woody wasn't a believer, and I knew he had been down that path before. However, Woody doesn't realize that Tommy truly believes in Jesus.

Tommy looked at Woody and said, "I have to return to Nam."

Woody asked, "When will that be?"

"I'm not sure," Tommy answered, "but it has to be soon."

He knew he needed to handle several details before leaving, such as getting a passport, organizing assistance for Woody, and planning his trip to Saigon.

Tommy did not know that Chi Le and their son had relocated to the Philippines. (Chi Le named their son Tommy Le, or T. Le.)

It would be difficult for her to leave the only place she knew and loved. Chi Le left Vietnam to seek asylum outside the country.

Political oppression, poverty, ongoing war, and the persecution of women with American children made Vietnam unsafe. Chi Le understood she had to leave because her son did not look Vietnamese, and she was labeled a supporter of the South. She feared her son T. Le's life.

When the war ended, T. Le was two years old. He was walking and beginning to speak English and Vietnamese, with some French mixed in.

Before he turned seven, he could speak four languages.

Chi Le was T. Le's first teacher. She taught him to read, solve math problems, and become academically competent. She talked to him, and they built a bond. Love and respect became a solid foundation.

It was April 30, 1975, and Saigon was under siege. The Viet Cong were making their way toward the Capitol building. The sound of bombs exploding nearby.

Chi Le knew she had to escape all the chaos and thought that when things calmed down, she and T. Le would return, but that would never happen. It would be the last time she would see the Saigon she knew and loved.

Chi Le did not know she would become one of the 130,000 Vietnamese refugees who fled their homeland.

This was the beginning of one of the most significant and prolonged refugee crises ever recorded. Between 1975 and 1997, over three million people escaped from Vietnam, Laos, and Cambodia.

Within two decades, they hungered for freedom and were willing to sacrifice their lives at sea; others sought refuge in camps in Thailand, Malaysia, or the Philippines. Over 2.5 million refugees were resettled worldwide, with over a million establishing new lives in the United States.

During this migration, Chi and T. Le would move to Puerto Princesa City, a village established in the western Philippines in the 1970s.

In 1977, T. Le was 4 years old, and he and his mother were forced to escape from Saigon. Chi Le did not know what she would do or where she would find work, but she understood that she had to leave Ho Chi Minh City (Saigon). She often wondered if she would ever see Tommy again.

She told T. Le about his father: "he was half Native American, Indiana, a Marine, a great, honest man who loved to carve wood and plant trees."

Chi Le and T Le leave Vietnam. Chi Le fears repercussions for supporting South Vietnam, falling in love with an American GI, and having his child. She and T Le are among many refugees leaving Saigon.

She seeks asylum and risks her life, with that of T Le. She boards a boat, not knowing where it is heading, but becoming one of the Boat People, determined to get out of Vietnam.

Many "boat people" did not survive as boats washed ashore in the northern Philippines.

Chi Le's boat was rescued by fishermen and other families living along the coast. Their vessels would drift aimlessly at sea before the current carries them to foreign waters.

Chi prays for the captain of the small boat, which is overcrowded and carried by the current.

"Would we live if you must take me, take me, and see that my baby is safe?"

Many boats were taken by the sea, but Chi's prayers were answered, and they drifted to the shore, greeted by people from the village.

The village was overcrowded, but Chi did not care; she and Tommy T. were on land and safe.

Note: In total, 2,700 refugees were admitted. They resided in the refugee processing centers in Ulagan Bay and Tara Island.

The Philippines has long been known for welcoming refugees. Its history is interesting because it has accepted refugees since 1927.

1.In 1927, at the end of World War I, the first wave of eight hundred "White Russians" arrived in the Philippines, fleeing persecution from "Red Russians" or supporters of the Socialist Revolution of 1917. These eight hundred Russians were part of a larger group of 7,000 to 8,000 refugees who escaped from Vladivostok City, one of the last military strongholds of the White Russians.

2.From 1934 to 1940, European Jews escaped Nazi persecution during World War II. One thousand two hundred Jewish refugees fled to the Philippines.

3.In 1939, Spanish republicans fleeing the aftermath of the Spanish Civil War joined the third wave of refugees.

4.In 1940, 30,000 Chinese immigrants sought refuge after the Chinese Civil War, aiming to evade the grasp of the newly formed communist People's Republic of China.

5.In 1947, the "Tiempo Ruso" (Time of the Russians) welcomed a second wave of 6,000 White Russians.

6.From 1975 to 1992, Vietnamese "boat people" or refugees fleeing the Vietnam War and reunification of North and South Vietnam made up the sixth wave.

7.At the close of the 1970s, the seventh wave arrived after the Iranian Revolution forced thousands of Iranians studying and working in Manila to seek refugee status in the Philippines instead of returning home to a new government that took over by force and violence.

8.Beginning in 1980, the eighth wave included nationals from other Asian countries fleeing regime changes in Laos, Cambodia, and Vietnam.

9.In 2000, a ninth wave consisted of East Timorese granted temporary protection during their country's struggle for independence from Indonesia. Approximately six hundred refugees from the Philippines' South Asian neighbors sought refuge in the country during this conflict.

Ref: *Nine Waves of Refugees in the Philippines – UNHCR Philippines*

Former President Estrada supported local fundraising efforts to assist the refugees. The Catholic Church in Manila raised $200,000 for the cause.

The refugees were granted permission to work, farm, and fish in the coastal village of Palawan.

Chi Le secured employment in fish cleaning but was not authorized to work outside the camp.

A considerable number of refugees opted to resettle in countries such as Canada.

Those who opted to remain initiated the establishment of a small community resembling Vietnam, which has become a local tourist attraction known as Viet Ville, developed on the premises of the former refugee camp.

Chi Le knew she could not return to Vietnam, her birthplace and the place she loved. Conflicted about whether to stay or immigrate to Canada, she was uncertain if she would ever see Tommy again or if he would ever meet their son.

She believed T Le would know as much about his father as she did.

She continued to write letters to Tommy, unsure if he would ever receive them. All the letters began with "Where are you?" She explained that she was carrying his child. She knew he wanted children and had already proposed to her, but she wondered, "Did I frighten him off?"

Tommy continues to write to Chi. Letters start coming back to him, _the address is unknown._ Now his mind begins to wander. _Is she dead?_

For both Tommy and Chi, days and nights seem to become longer. Chi began having sleepless nights, and Tommy continued to sleep with one eye open.

Their love for one another seems to be cemented with the strongest bond ever invented by man.

Dear Tommy

Where are you? We have a son, Tommy T., born on April 15, 1973. He is the joy of my life. He looks a lot like you, pure beautiful complexion, blue eyes, dark hair, and a smile that will capture the world; he is perfectly my pearl from the sea.

I must leave now, Love Chi,

All letters received from Chi to Tommy were kept at the Military Post Office and years after the war ended, they would be sent to Tommy.

Chapter 11

What was happening at home?

In or around 1968, the anti-war movement began in the homeland. Articles like "U.S. soldiers had mercilessly slaughtered more than 400 unarmed civilians in the village of My Lai did not help." The anti-war protests continued to grow as the conflict wore on. In 1968 and 1969, there were hundreds of protest marches and gatherings in America.

November 15, 1969, marked the largest anti-war march in American history. It occurred in Washington, D.C., with approximately 250,000 protesters gathering peacefully to demand the end of the war and the withdrawal of American troops.

Many college campuses became highly active in the anti-war movement and started to divide Americans. For young students, the war represented a form of unchecked government that they came to resent.

While American military personnel were engaged in intense combat in the rice fields and jungles of Vietnam, significant social upheaval transpired across the United States.

Citizens commenced vocalizing their discontent from the West Coast to the East Coast. In public spaces, on university campuses, and through various media coverage, widespread criticism of the war began to illuminate the inaccuracies conveyed to the American public. Discussions regarding the potential reinstatement of the draft resonated in both the

streets and on campus: "HELL NO WE WON'T GO."
The protest grew in intensity over the years.

May 2025 – Netflix – "Turning Point"
This documentary series depicts the human cost associated with the prolonged conflict in which America was engaged. Some have praised its in-depth explanation of the war, while others criticized its focus on anti-war sentiment and its portrayal of fairness and balance. They feel it unfairly blames veterans and focuses too heavily on anti-war sentiment, overlooking the sacrifices and dedication of those who served.

In 1972, the first U.S. military unit began to withdraw. However, those who remain grew increasingly angry, frustrated, and confused. Problems with morale and leadership started to multiply. During this time, thousands of troops received dishonorable discharges for desertion.

Back in the States, over 500,000 men became "draft dodgers," with many fleeing to Canada.

The draft ended in 1972 under President Nixon, and an all-volunteer army became a reality the following year.

In 1970, the campus of Kent State University became the site of a protest that will never be forgotten.

The U.S. and South Vietnamese armies invaded Cambodia, hoping to eradicate the DRV supply bases. Subsequently, the South led its invasion of Laos, which the North met and pushed back.

The invasion of these nations breached international laws, triggering a fresh surge of college campus protests throughout America.

On May 4, 1970, at Kent State University in Ohio, National Guardsmen shot and killed four students. Just ten days later, police shot two students at Jackson State University in Mississippi.

In June 1972, after a failed offensive in South Vietnam, Hanoi was finally willing to compromise. Kissinger and North Vietnamese representatives drafted a peace agreement by early fall, but leaders in Saigon rejected it.

In December, Nixon authorized the bombing of Hanoi and Haiphong. Known as the Christmas Bombings, the bombings drew international criticism.

Vietnam War: Causes, Facts & Impact - HISTORY
The Pentagon Papers:

Daniel Ellsberg leaked the Pentagon Papers in 1971. This name refers to a top-secret Department of Defense study of U.S. political and military involvement in Vietnam from 1945 to 1967.

Ellsberg, who had worked on the study, opposed the war and decided that the American people should know about the information in the Pentagon Papers.

In March 1971, he provided a photocopy to The New York Times. The Times subsequently published a series of scathing articles based on the report, which had been kept secret.
Ref: *Pentagon Papers - HISTORY*

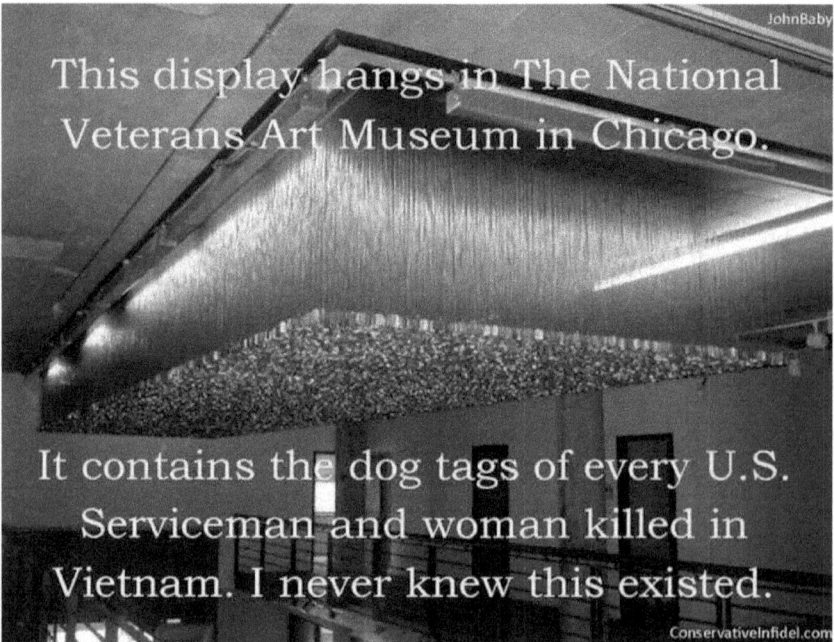

This display hangs in The National Veterans Art Museum in Chicago. It contains the dog tags of every U.S. Serviceman and woman killed in Vietnam. I never knew this existed.

Our involvement in the conflict was characterized by confusion, as we lacked clarity regarding our presence, yet our servicemen and women persevered until the conclusion.

Approximately 50,000 individuals did not return, leading to mistrust in our government and to question why the war was not concluded.

For numerous individuals, it appeared to be an interminable struggle. Veterans returning from Vietnam did not experience the celebratory fanfare afforded to those returning from World War II.

Instead, they returned to a nation deeply divided by contentious debates surrounding the war. There were no parades or welcoming rallies; instead, they met with indifference, and it seemed as though the sacrifices they endured in Vietnam were disregarded.

Veterans encountered challenges in reintegrating into society, resorting to substances such as drugs and alcohol to mitigate their suffering. Additionally, the government failed to support these individuals, not fulfilling the commitments made to those who served.

Veterans returning home encountered a negative instinctual response and bureaucratic obstacles.

Consequently, veterans like Tommy T. and others were left to ponder the significance of their service and its actual impact.

Dear Chi

I'm back in the States, and even though I am not welcomed this is the only home I know. This is my birthplace and the place I dream of bringing you. Times will change like the seasons, and I will fit in, many will never know I served as a Marine, I killed because I was told to. I will never regret being a Marine.

Love Triple T.

Chapter 12
Tommy T. goes to Ho Chi Minh City. (Saigon)

In May 1980, all arrangements had been made for Tommy to return to Vietnam. Woody would take over the business, and Tommy explained to him to run it as he feels it should be run. "If I don't return everything, it belongs to you. - All paperwork has been filed with his attorney." Just take care of others. Woody has been with Tommy for over 12 years and knows how Tommy thinks and gives. He understands Gramps' philosophy because he has heard it and lived it for 12 years. During that time, they took in other veterans such as Mad Dog Williams and a homeless vet, and did the same for him as was done for Woody. Mad Dog has been with them for 10 years. After Mad Dog came No Teeth Holmes, who had a rough journey with painkillers and suffered from PTSD. After No Teeth, they took in One Eye Marshall, whom they called The Sheriff. Along with Mad Dog and The Marshall came their wives and children. The valley became a self-sufficient village, living according to Gramps's philosophy.

Tommy shares with Woody, Mad Dog Williams, No Teeth Holmes, and One Eye Marshall the core of Gramps' philosophy, which is vital for teaching people to coexist peacefully. This philosophy would become the constitution of their village. The words of harmony would foster hope and blessings. To this day, it reminds every one of his grandfather's Indian teachings, which stress their duty to be devoted to God and care for others. Tommy deeply loves the Indiana Way, envisioning a better world if we emulated the peaceful Indians instead of the wicked ones.

He values nature's essence and the wisdom it offers for daily living. His experiences in Vietnam solidified his belief that the horrors of unnecessary violence opened him to Indian philosophy, highlighting mankind's role in bettering the world. He views this as a daily obligation and insists we no longer ignore the world due to greed and ignorance, failing to appreciate the beauty of collaboration. This perspective refers to the Garden of Eden, advocating for a respectful and strong commitment to caring for God's creations.

Tommy lives by the philosophy of his grandfather. "How to be a man."

1. Being a man involves more than just age; it requires knowledge that broadens the mind and soul. It demands that you listen to your elders and follow their way of life.

2. He valued rising early and going to bed early. Wake up with the sunrise and maintain a positive mindset. Avoid procrastination when tasks need attention. Prioritize what is essential. Comment on the body and soul regarding the teachings of God. Understanding God's will be better than seeking to be understood. Therefore, focus on working rather than talking.

3. Each day, remind yourself to live for God, not just for your purpose. While others may share similar journeys or accompany you, the responsibility to shape your future lies within you.

4. Never be rude to a neighbor or someone you meet along the way, and always ensure they receive the best you can offer—this includes food, drink, land, and, most importantly, friendship.

5. Nothing belongs to you unless you have earned it. Respect other people's property, and don't decide anything for yourself that you don't deserve.

6. Listen to those who have not found their way, and treat them with kindness, love, and respect. We can be quick to judge when others don't follow our path. It is your responsibility to guide them through your actions.

7. Respect and care for what God has given us. Never mistreat a plant, animal, or person. These are gifts from God and should be treated as such.

8. Never speak about someone in a harmful way or behind their back. People enjoy spreading gossip and find it amusing. Don't spread negative energy; use your energy to promote positivity.

9. Forgive those who trespass against you. Every person makes mistakes, and we must forgive quickly when someone makes a judgment based on their life experiences that are less beneficial than ours.

10. View the world as a beautiful place and contribute positively. Negative thinking can harm your mental well-being, body, and spirit, trapping you in a hellish state of being. Your purpose is to cultivate positive thoughts and maintain the right attitude toward things that matter.

11. The land and all its creatures are part of the Earth that sustains us and belong to no one.

12. Teach our children to develop great minds. Treat them well, for they are the future.

13. You must share this: if you see a person in need, feed him, clothe him, and shelter him. Giving back is the most essential characteristic of a man.

Note – Before departing from Chi Le, Tommy wrote down these principles for her and encouraged her to read them, asking if she could embrace these rules, principles, or philosophies—however we wish to define them. Chi Lee stayed up late, absorbing the principles, and in the morning, she told Tommy, "Yes, I can, and I will live by them starting today." Tommy embraced her, lifting her slightly so they were face-to-face, and with tears in his eyes, he said, "If you believe, then we are married. We will have a church wedding when I return."

Tommy sat and wondered whether he was doing the right thing. He asked himself: Should I return to search for Chi Le? Would she remember me? Is she married, and does she have a family? Will I find her? Tommy knew one thing for sure: These questions needed to be answered. He understood he had to try because he loved her.

Tommy traveled to his spiritual sanctuary in the mountains, seeking guidance from the Gods about whether he was on the right path and if they would respond. After collecting some dry wood, he lit a fire and spread out his blanket on the ground to sit and pray for answers. He spotted an eagle and realized this could be the greatest honor he could receive: a feather from either a Golden or a Bald Eagle. Soon after, a red fox appeared before him. In Native American culture, the red fox is regarded as a sacred creature. Most tribes view the fox as a trickster, celebrated for its cleverness and skill in evading predators. Additionally, the fox symbolizes good fortune and often serves as a revered spirit guide. Just as he started to drift off, the sound of a rattlesnake's rattle stirred him. The rattlesnake represents strength, power, and transformation; for many tribes, it signifies new beginnings. It also served as a reminder to remain cautious. As Tommy's eyes fluttered open, he contemplated how the Gods would continue guiding him. When he turned towards the morning sun, he discovered an eagle feather placed firmly at his side.

Tommy began to break up camp and saw a mother bear playing with her cub. Most tribes show great respect for bears. Bears symbolize authority, good medicine, courage, and strength at their core. Like a mother bear protecting her young, it is said that leaders who possess bear medicine stand up for what is right and fight for what is good.

Tommy felt his questions were answered, and the spiritual Gods encouraged him to begin his journey. Arrangements have been made, and Tommy T. is ready for a new journey.

Chapter 13

Arrival of Tommy T. in Laos Long Tieng Airfield, Laos, Vietnam

Long Tieng Airfield, Laos, Vietnam

From 1968 to 1974, Long Tieng Airfield, located in Laos, operated as a bustling airport. It served as a significant United States military base in Laos, utilized for various operations, including the evacuation of refugees to Canada, the United States, the Philippines, Guam, and other locations. It was also identified as the CIA's Secret War, which they called Lima Site 20A.

The base was abandoned in 1975 and is currently recognized as Wat Mai International Airport. Going through customs, he spoke only Vietnamese, as clearly and fluently as a native. Also processing a Passport from Vietnam with the name Tommy Le.

In the early morning, Tommy arrives in Laos, skeptical, knowing he has to fly to an airport controlled by the communists. Although he never ventured this far north during his time in Vietnam, he is familiar with Laos, Hanoi, and Ha Long Bay. While Tommy feels uneasy about not being in uniform, he understands that he is significantly safer by not drawing attention to his military involvement.

Tommy begins to visit and re-visit his reasoning and questions his thoughts.

. Will I ever find her?

. Is she married?

. Am I doing the right thing?

. Will she feel the same as I do?

. Did I wait too long?

. Is she alive?

Tommy arrived in Laos in mid-June after departing the USA in early May 1980 with a two-passport and plenty of cash. Not knowing much about the banking system in Vietnam, he decided to carry a money belt filled with cash. Red tape and delays led him to believe he would never find his true love, Chi Lee.

Not wanting to bring attention to himself, he stays in a hotel, fit for fleas and rats. You might wonder why he chose to fly to Laos. He attempted to book a flight to what used to be Saigon but found it challenging to secure an international flight without several layovers. Ultimately, he figured it would be much more efficient to head to Laos instead and travel south.

Sitting in his small, dirty hotel room, he begins to write a letter to Chi.

Dear Chi,

I know it has been quite a journey for you, and I wanted to reach out again. Can you believe I am in Laos, getting ready to head to Saigon? I look forward to visiting all those special places we explored, where you worked, and where we lived. I am determined to find you!
I will try to find Sister Mary at the sisters' home; I will visit the BBQ where you worked like a slave for the North. I am sure our home is still in our name, or at least that is what I heard the last time I spoke with Ho Loe, my friend in Nam.

I know you are alive because I can see you in my dreams, running joyfully with someone. I hope and pray that it is not your husband; if it is, I would be happy for you, but I would still carry many scars in my heart. I even dreamed of you on a motor scooter, zipping through the jungle, and I do not know why, but my dreams, as I believe, are a message to me from the God of dreams.

My visions come and go, like the wind lifting a leaf from the ground and carrying it hundreds of miles away from its location, and then it starts another journey.

I do not know how to get this letter to you, so that being known, I will mail it myself. I hope you will be able to read it someday.

Love, TTT

To maintain a low profile, Tommy took a job with a cargo container company to travel back to Ho Chi Minh City, formerly known as Saigon. Thanks to his fluency in different languages, he was assigned the supervisor role and reported directly to the captain, overseeing a dedicated team of workers. The journey itself turned out to be relatively routine, but it provided him with opportunities to listen and learn about the migration of Vietnamese people to the Philippines. Once back in Ho Chi Minh City, he realized he needed to arrange transportation to the Philippines.

Unfortunately, he found no information on Chi Lee in Ho Chi Minh City. Eager to help, he visited every agency that assisted refugees in finding new homes abroad, but she seemed nowhere to be found despite all his efforts.

Trust was a scarce commodity on board the vessel. Tommy wandered despite having sufficient funds to purchase the ship. He preferred not to draw attention to himself. He endeavored to blend in with the local populace and achieved remarkable success. He deliberately avoided eye contact when he could but gave eye contact as a supervisor. He communicated in the assimilated language without any discernible accent. His linguistic skills were acquired by Chi Le, who considered it imperative that he speak without an accent.

Once in Ho Chi Minh City, Tommy tried to secure passage to the Philippines. Records of refugees were not maintained, and many refugees used fake paperwork, making it impossible to locate the person he was searching for. Tommy knew all about counterfeit passports.

Dead or alive, Tommy was convinced he would find Chi. He began to debate whether he should travel to the Philippines, but he realized he needed to get back to the States and was losing faith in his mission.

While Tommy traveled down the coast of the South China Sea, Chi Le tried to arrange for herself and T Le to travel to Canada. Chi Le had limited funds. She took on odd jobs to raise enough money, but she would never sacrifice her body or sell the gold watch her father gave her. Chi Le was a beautiful woman whom strange men always approached. However, she was devoted to one man and one man only.

Chi knew how to take care of herself! During her time at the Catholic school, she took required self-defense classes. This class taught her a martial arts form of self-defense, and Chi proudly earned her black belt, which is seen as the highest level. Yet, for those who truly wish to master art, it is just the beginning of an exciting journey to a more advanced level of study. Chi kept working on her skills even after graduation! Her goal was to go all the way. This is how she is; she believes that if you are going to commit to something, you go all the way.

Her goa a red belt with white strips, further representing the highest degree of black belt. After the 4th degree black belt, which she has not mastered, she plans to achieve the 5th to 10th degree black belt.

Tommy T. is often seen sharpening his skills with high kicks and hard hits to a hanging workout bag.

When asked why she puts so much effort into everything, Chi replies, "Because that is the way I was raised." She genuinely wants to give Tommy T. all the opportunities possible. Having come from a wealthy family and lost everything, she feels grateful that her parents instilled valuable survival skills in her.

"I am sure Triple T knows how to behave and not upset her." As she practices, so does Tommy T, who is now a first-level black—at least, that is what Chi believes. She does not have the money to further his classes.

Chapter 14
The Journey

She was determined to find the man she loved. Still in the Philippines, she continued to look for a way to Canada.

The Refugee Act of 1980 established the U.S. refugee resettlement program and granted asylum to individuals like Chi Le. To protect her from persecution, her name was changed to Kathy Lee Johnson, and her son's name was altered to Tom Lee Johnson. The Act also created the Office of Refugee Resettlement to oversee refugee admissions and the reset-tlement program. However, her documents were filed under Kathy Lee Johnson, making locating her as Chi Le impossible.

(Chi Le) Kathy did not travel to Canada, but the US government would fly her to San Francisco and then to New York City, where she planned to find a job and an apartment in the Bronx. She was thankful for her ability to speak Vietnamese, English, French, and various dialects of Chinese. Due to her language skills, it was easy for her to secure a job. Consequently, she became a translator at the Immigration Office. She found a place to live in the Bronx, and Tom Lee became a Yankees fan.

Tom, like most young men, loves playing baseball. Tommy is passionate about sports and dreams of playing in the MLB someday. He envisions himself at the bottom of the ninth inning at the plate, with the game tied. With grace, he lifts his bat to rest beside his baby's soft skin. He lifts the bat from his shoulder, settles into a baseball stance, swings, and makes direct contact with the ball as it soars over the left field fence. As he listens to the crowd's roar, he circles the bases, holding his hat over his head and encouraging the audience. (Just like Bill Mazeroski for the Pittsburgh Pirates' win over the Yankees in 1960,)

T. Le will soon turn eight and is already 5'9" tall, a trait he inherited from his father. Chi Le is also relatively tall for a Vietnamese woman. Wher-ever they spent time on their journey, T. Le could find other boys to play sports with; they usually played soccer, baseball, and basketball. T. Le ex-celled in sports, was a great reader, and enjoyed American Literature and American Indian folklore. He also excelled in mathematics and science. Chi Le insisted that T. Le study and attend classes whenever possible. Education was not always available, so T. Le was home-schooled. He re-ceived a half-hour of playtime for every four hours spent learning; after lessons, he would be allowed an hour of playtime.

Remember, Chi was at one of the best schools in Vietnam, and the Chris-tian Academy was known for its excellence in teaching. By the time she graduated, she was considered equal to a college junior. Her ability in math, literature, and language was far superior to that of many college graduates.

Dear Tommy

I hope and pray you get this letter. I haven't heard from you, and knowing how much you loved me, I am certain you have not received any letters. Your son and I are in San Francisco (USA), waiting for our papers to depart for New York City. If all goes well, I will have a job waiting for me. I will be working at the Immigration Office processing Vietnamese refugees. I am excited that our son will attend public school for the first time. He is a great son whom I am very proud of. He listens and obeys the rules. Establishing guidelines, like my parents did for me, is very important. I believe you are now a civilian and in the USA. Looking forward to embracing your body.

Love

Chi

Chapter 15
Settling in the USA.

While Chi Le demonstrated her skills and efficiency at the Immigration Office, Tom T. thrived academically and excelled in multiple sports such as soccer, baseball, track, and basketball. He soon recognized that he was smarter, faster, and more athletic than most, if not all his classmates. Chi Le made sure her son stayed humble and grounded. Every Sunday, Tom T. and Chi Le went to a lovely nearby church, where she treasured the warmth and uplifting emotions experienced during and after the services.

Their simple apartment was a short walk from both the school and Chi Le's workplace. A small park nearby featured a basketball court and various activities that Tom T. often enjoyed. Nevertheless, the rule remained: prioritize schoolwork first, and if time allowed, you could go play with your friends.

Chi expressed amazement at the multitude of items available at the market, as well as the substantial number of street vendors present. She harbored concerns that certain Vietnamese individuals who had established residence in this area might be spies. She exhibited caution towards all individuals, particularly those of Russian and Turkish descent.

She felt an overwhelming sense of joy and gratitude. For the first time, her son could attend a public school just a short walk away! Tommy displayed academic skills beyond his years, excelling in mathematics, science, literature, and foreign languages. He was wonderfully skilled in English, French, Vietnamese, Russian, and Chinese. His impressive language abilities meant he could help translate for many of his class-mates, as over half of the class were refugees. He was all set to attend the Diamond Heights School in the Bronx for International Students, and everyone was excited for him!

His basketball skills are reflected in a superstar like Jim Curry in the NBA! Playing sports came to him as effortlessly as his academic achievements did. Everyone who knew him affectionately called him "the natural."

T. J. got out of bed early and began preparing for his first day at public school. He was not worried but concerned about how he would be ac-cepted, having a Vietnamese mother and half-bred American father. He wasn't worried about being bullied because of his size and skills in Viet-namese wrestling, which is known as Dau Vet. It is a traditional martial art and cultural practice with a history spanning over 1,000 years. T.J. would learn that his mother knew a lot about USA teen dress. She ob-served what the young men were wearing.

During this time, schools in NYC became wonderful places for learners to build strong social bonds and discover their identities. Sports were the unifying force for communities, where it felt like race didn't matter if you celebrated a victory together. There were so many extracurric-ular activities to choose from, and students were drawn to them with enthusiasm. Just think, this was all before the era of video games and the internet!

In the 1970s, the New York Knicks featured a world champion starting lineup, including superstars Walt Frazier, Earl (the Peral) Monroe, Bill Bradley, Dave DeBusschere, and Willis Reed. The New York Knicks, one of the NBA's oldest franchises, won two NBA titles in 1970 & in the year T, Lee was born1973.

Tommy encountered a young man his age named JoJo at a crosswalk as he walked to school. JoJo was shorter than Tommy, with a book bag tossed over his shoulder, a basketball tucked under his arm, and great shoes. His smile was so bright it could light up the night sky! They both looked at one another and smiled with a nod of the head. Tommy J.

knew he would be okay.

During this period, a child of black and white parents was commonly referred to as mulatto. Nowadays, this word is considered offensive and outdated. A more likely term used is biracial. The letters "M or 'B" may appear on most forms that ask for race. Tommy T. often wonders why "H" is not used for humans.

T. J. exchanged class locations with JoJo to learn that they would share the same homeroom and attend the same first class, American History.

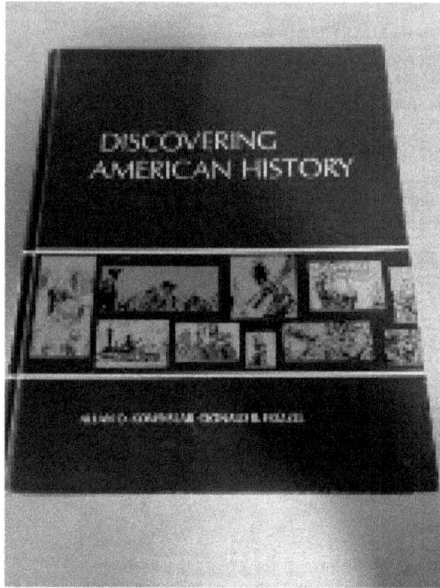

The text was "Discovering American History" by Holt, Rinehart, and Winston. They gave a copy and explained not to mark it up or pay $5.00 to buy it. Knowing how short cash was, he would take care of it and wrap it. With the help of JoJo, they wrapped all their books in brown paper grocery bags.

Woo, T. J. thought he had never seen so many different skin colors in one room/sitting together: white, black, yellow, and red. However, thank God there was no green. Everyone respected each other and treated each other the way they should be treated. Most were on similar journeys to get to America.

T.J. soon learned that many students did not possess the academic skills he had, and for that moment, he felt very proud of his mother for pushing him to study. After testing T.J., it was recommended that he advance a few grades. However, his mother believed it best for him to remain in the assigned grade.

Chi explains that she would be uncomfortable knowing her son was with older and more experienced students in areas her son was not ready for. She felt he would adjust to the situation just like any normal child. However, because of his athletic skills, he would play basketball with the older students. No one could play as well as Tommy T when on the court.

In the ninth grade, T. stood six feet three inches tall and would grow another three inches before graduation. JoJo began calling him T. soon after they met, and the name "stuck. T. stood out in both the classroom and on the basketball court. T. began calling JoJo J., and the name stuck. T. and J. would become friends for a lifetime. They bonded with trust and respect and shared thoughts they would tell no one else, especially their parents. When they needed support, they knew who to turn to. They would celebrate each other's joy and be there during rough times. They valued one another's opinions and feelings.

T and J spoke for hours about their backgrounds and soon learned more about each other than they had ever thought possible. They were now blood brothers.

Chapter 16
JoJo, Jesse, and Sue

His father grew up in the Bronx, NYC, and served in the Army during the Vietnam War. He wed Sue while still in the service, and after his discharge, they relocated to the Bronx. JoJo described his mother as a gentle, caring person who loved him more than she loved herself. She supported South Vietnam, and because of her support, she needed to leave Vietnam. Her marriage and having a child facilitated her move to America. Unfortunately, she lost her parents in a bombing during the war. The city was hit hard, and many lost everything. There were hundreds of casualties from both sides.

His father (Jesse Jackson) was a tall, good-looking man with blue eyes that no woman could resist. He met Sue and after a few dates he knew he was in love. Shortly after, they were married. When JoJo was born, they knew they had to get to the States, where JoJo would have more opportunities. Both were church-going individuals and were married in a Catholic church.

Jesse was part of many battles and did not trust the American government. Like many other GIs, he began to question what was happening in Vietnam. The Battle of Hue was the worst-fought, significantly influencing the growth of anti-war sentiment at home and in Vietnam.

The battle, which transpired during January and February of 1968, is regarded as one of the deadliest confrontations of the war. It occurred in the city where Sue had resided before her evacuation to a smaller town south of the city. Sue could stay in her residence because this segment of the town was not directly involved in the combat. Nevertheless, the battle resulted in a significant number of casualties on both sides, including many women and children.

One can only imagine the war taking place in the streets where you grew up, seeing the buildings destroyed, making it brutal and challenging for everyone. The capture of Hue, the capital of Vietnam, was a major and strategic victory for the US and ARVN forces but also came at a very high cost.

Jesse was among the numerous individuals injured during the battle. The 95th Evacuation Hospital, located in Da Nang, served as the primary medical facility throughout the war. This institution provided comprehensive medical care to all service members. The hospital specifically attended to the wounded during the Battle of Hue.
The war was not nice, but what war ever was? There were many with severe burns, broken bones, shrapnel wounds, brain injuries, spinal cord injuries, nerve damage, paralysis, loss of sight, and hearing. Post-traumatic stress disorder (PTSD) and limb loss. Imagine one of your loved ones returning to a tomato, rotten egg-throwing welcome home in the USA.

Jessee was wounded from shrapnel, which would leave him walking with the support of a cane and in pain. PTSD began to bring back memories, which left him angry and challenged his family to be around him. Sometimes, it was difficult for JoJo to comprehend, but Sue knew what she had to deal with and became his caretaker for life.

Shrapnel wounds varied in severity, with some leading to limb loss or many other complications. Jesse was not hit in the head, where many people die as a result. His spinal cord was not damaged, but he suffered from nerve damage, leaving him weak, in pain, and with a loss of feeling in his left hand. Jesse also suffered from hearing loss, and his disorder led to a significant psychological impact of the war.

At first, Sue did not know if he was living. Without the means to get around the city, no phone, electricity, or public transportation, she did what she had to: walk. She knew it would be a long journey, some 300 miles, but she also knew she had to know one way or another. Leaving Hue with a backpack containing food, a blanket, her Bible, and warm clothes, she left the city. The hospital was approximately 70 miles from Hue.

Walking for a day, Sue arrives outside the village of "A Luoi. She finds a secure location near the road but well camouflaged in the forest. She eats dry food and sets her blanket down to sleep. She returns to her journey in the morning, heading south to Vinh Moc. She would find shelter in the lovely home of her cousin, a fisherman who owns his own boat. She would share a meal with her cousin's family, noodles, rice, and fish served in bowls with chopsticks. Her cousin would give her use of his motor scooter, which would enable her to reach the hospital in an hour. In Khe Sanb, a small mountain village, she encounters some North Vietnamese militants who attempt to hijack her scooter and her belongings. As she approaches the militants, she must make a life-risking decision. Should I stop or try to escape on a scooter through the jungle? She sees a path through the jungle and decides to take the risk. This path must have been used by many Vietnamese who were escaping somewhere.

Under intense gunfire, she started running from the militants. Being chased by a truck and machine gun, she manages to navigate a hillside where the truck hits a rock and flips over. However, she keeps riding like a maniac to escape. Now, I am lost and do not know which way to go. She thinks, I am heading south, the sun sets in the west. I will travel south until I see a safe place.

She is unaware that she is only a few miles from the hospital. In the morning, she saw helicopters flying above and knew they were USA helicopters. She meets a family traveling on foot to Da Nang, and after giving them food and water, she continues her journey.

Arriving at the hospital, she encounters hundreds of people looking for military and civilian loved ones. More than three hundred beds and some five hundred patients are waiting in the wings. A third portable hospital is under construction to manage the overflow. The process takes hours. Sue sleeps on the floor along with others until the morning. She still does not know if Jesse is alive.

Confused and frustrated, she tries to locate Jesse but continues without success. She travels hallway after hallway and now thinks she must visit the morgue. Terrified, she begins to travel to a tent area where they house the dead. As she begins to cross the field, she hears someone calling her name. Not knowing what direction it is coming from, she starts swirling in circles and sees Jesse being carried on a stretcher towards the hospital.

Sue sprints across the field, her heart swelling with joy when she spots Jesse. To her, it looks like he is wrapped in white bandages, covering his body from head to toe. His face is covered with a white mesh, gently protecting his skin from the sun and any burns. The doctor advises her not to touch him, but she can walk beside him as they make their way to the hospital together. Jesse received treatment in the field, as his injuries weren't as severe as those of the other troops. All Sue could think was how grateful she was that he was alive, thanking God that he was home and safe.

She only uttered, over a hundred times, "Jesse, I am here." At his side, she demonstrated pure unconditional love for her light skin, blue eyes, red hair, and black man. Now you can imagine what their offspring will look like.

Jesse could hear his wife as she expressed her worries, but he also felt a sense of relief in her voice. He thought, how difficult it must have been for her.

He knew he would soon return to the States and wondered how that would be. He wanted to return to the Bronx, NYC.

Larry Green wrote an article for the Daily News in 1972 explaining the brutality of the War.

Private Pham Van Le

Bien Hoa, South Vietnam – Pham Van Le had just completed his military training on Sunday, bravely stepped into combat on Monday, and tragically lost his life on Tuesday, with his final resting place being Saturday. He was only 23 years old, married for seven joyful months, and was a dedicated porter at the Saigon docks before being drafted.

On that day, he was among a dozen others laid to rest, interred each day in this somber National Cemetery, where sorrow is unending and the ranks of soldiers bring no special honors. Family members, including his beloved wife, mother, father, and sister, gathered to say their good-byes.

For hours, the women grieved deeply, their cries echoing in anguish as they denounced the government for sending him to war, desperately pleading for him to come back to them.

They lived in houses and drove cars; they worked in offices. "Those old men don't die, only the young!" shouted his 19-year-old widow amidst the sounds of other mourners at various funerals.

These families struggled, having moved countless times in search of safety from the conflict. "My son, my son, I am here to see you. You used to take me everywhere. Why don't you take me with you?" his heartbroken mother lamented.

Informal honor guards then marched to the coffin, carrying it to a black military van. They accompanied it with dignity in this brief farewell procession through the field of freshly dug graves. There was one final opportunity to bid farewell as the wife and mother threw themselves over the coffin.

As the gravedigger filled the grave, the black van arrived, delivering the next body while the unfilled graves baked under the sun. "My husband, my husband, they permitted my husband to die."

He was one of over 8,000 South Vietnamese soldiers lost. More than 25,000 graves await.

Would Chi and Tommy ever connect?

They both are beginning to feel it is a lost cause, but neither will give up because of the love embedded in their hearts and souls.

Tommy purchases an old scooter outside Saigon. He pays fifty American dollars for it, three times the dong's value. This is like gold to the seller due to the higher return rate.

Tommy returns to the Catholic Home, finding it dire need repairs. The Home appears abandoned. Shutters hanging from the windows are broken, the ground needs care, and weeds and trees grow freely. Tommy slowly navigates the ground on roads torn by military tanks and other vehicles. His eye catches something moving on the upper floor. He parks the scooter and walks up toward the door, and someone yells, "We are the sisters and want no trouble, we are unarmed. Just then, a sister walks from home, arms over her head. Tommy replies, "I am looking for Sister Mary," and Sister Grace replies, "She passed on after being shot by rebels." Tommy thought my only means of learning more about Chi. And she is dead. Sister Grace, a few years older than Chi, asked, "Can I help you?" Tommy replies, "Perhaps, I am looking for a young lady named Chi Le. Oh, respond, Grace. I knew Chi Le; she lived in the home after graduating and waited tables at a restaurant in Saigon City. Are you Tommy, her fiancé?" Yes, I'm Tommy. "Can you help me?"

Sister Grace responds, "I am not sure, so many were killed, beheaded, rapped, left in the street to be eaten by dogs. I don't mean to destroy your hopes, but I have seen too much killing, and I am only here because Jesus has more planned for me.

Tommy begins to tear up at the thought that Chi was tortured in such a brutal way. Sister Grace asks Tommy, "May I offer you a meal, something to drink, water perhaps?" Tommy replies, "I am okay; however, Chi asked me to give this gift to you. " Five fresh one-hundred-dollar bills are folded in his hand. He extends his hand to shake hers, touching their hands as Tommy slips the gift into her hand.

Tommy, "May I ask you something, and please don't say yes, or no? Until you think about it. We have an orphan boy with us; if he stays here, he will have no future. Can you see if you can take him home to the USA with you?"

Tommy replies, "Let me think about it. I will ask my Gods and Jesus for answers. I will pray and listen for answers. The first thing he thought about was that he always wanted children, which may be the answer, but he thought again, how?

"Tommy said he would return in a few days with an answer," Sister Grace responded. That is all I ask. May your Gods respond quickly. I am sure they will talk to Jesus.

As Tommy drove away, he thought, "I am glad she did tell me his name, because I know how attached I get, and knowing his name would create a deeper image.

Before he got to the road, he knew the answer: I would take this boy with me if possible. I am sure Woody would appreciate the company. The big question was How?

Tommy locates the BBQ where he met Chi and fell in love. It didn't look as welcoming as it once did. He was leery of going in. He waited outside, hoping to see someone he knew, but luck wasn't with him. He walked to the back and saw someone bring out trash, he looked familiar with his ball cap turned to the side. Tommy parked his scooter and approached the man. The dishwasher said, "If you are looking for a handout, you came to the wrong place."

In Vietnamese, Tommy said, "No, I'm looking for honest information." The dishwasher said, "Honest, you won't find that here, but I will give you what I can; just ask." Tommy asked, "How many years have you worked here?" Tee responded, "Over 20." Tommy said, "Have you ever met a waitress named Chi?" Tee responded, "How much cash do you have?" Toomy gave him a pocket of Vietnamese coins.

Tee responded, "NO," and began walking away. "You mean Sweet Tea Le?" Tommy said, "Yes, I believe that is what they called her." Tommy quickly handed him some money in exchange for information. Tee said, "She was a beautiful lady who respected everyone. She treated me with dignity and made me feel important. She once told me she could not do her job if it weren't for me, and I asked what, and she said we need clean dishes." That made me feel needed. I can't say if she is dead or alive; she wanted to escape to Canada or America. Not only was she beautiful, but she was smart. I believe she had a university education." Tommy hands him a few more Vietnamese dollars. Tee said please be careful, I could be killed for this. They call it treason. Tommy replies, "I will see you tomorrow."

The next day, Tee meets Tommy and tells Tommy, "She may have escaped to America during a military evacuation around 1975.

If she stayed, she would be dead, because she would be considered a trader. I got by because I always kept my mouth shut, but only Chi respected what a dishwasher had to say." Tommy asks Tee, "Where can I go for more information?" Tee explains that he "believes some religious group that runs an underground organization, and he would see what he could do." He also told Tommy that some were escaping to Hong Kong and Singapore.

Tommy returns to see Sister Grace to explain that he will do everything in his power to take the boy with him, but he refuses to meet him because he fears he will love him the moment he sees him, just like he loved Woody at first sight.

Sister Grace explains, "Many children are called 'children of dust, and face many hardships living in the streets. They were abandoned and left to starve; they struggle with discrimination due to their mixed race and live in conditions that aren't fit for a rat.

She goes on to say that the American government is concerned about the fate of these children and is leading to new laws and policies aimed at 5 for them, but she is not clear.

Little did they know that the Asian American Immigration law was passed to expedite the children. It was next to impossible for Sister Grace to find their father, mother, or any extended family, and she did not have the funds to do that.
]
Information can be found in a Dartmouth Study, taken in 2014, which was launched the same year. It was an oral history project that interviewed Dartmouth and Upper Valley communities. They listened and recorded their experiences in Vietnam from 1950 through 1975,

Chapter 17
Big decision

Triple T had a difficult time trying to sleep. He envisioned himself as a bee trapped in a bottle and kept trying to get out. He felt he was imprisoned and had nowhere to go. As he lay sleepless, he began to ask himself what Gramps would do. Confused, his mind became clear as he knew what Gramps would do.

"He thought, where do I go? His first stop would be to visit an attorney. His first question was "Is our interview private and only between you and me.

He was visiting Ty Van Yen's office. He addressed him by his first name because that is proper in Vietnam.

Triple T. spoke in Vietnamese. Ty assured him that the conversation would be private, and the initial discussion was free and private.

Triple T asked, "Can I record our conversation?"

Ty said, "Yes," as he responded to Triple T,

"That is what I wanted to hear, and decided he did not need to record." Triple T. explained that he spoke to Sister Grace at the old orphanage. He explains that a mixed-race American boy is being harbored at the Home with Sister Grace.

I want to take him back to the States with me. Ty says,

"Oh, you are American. Can we speak in English? "Triple T, you speak perfect Vietnamese."

"Thank you, responds TTT

"I have doubts because this government is not cooperative, especially with Americans with issues. Ty goes on to say, I will see what we can do.

Triple T, ask "How much do I owe you?

Ty responds, "Nothing.

I explained that the first visit is free, and even if it were not, I would charge you nothing because I appreciate your journey."

TTT ask? When can we visit again?

Ty responds, "Give me two days, and just show up early." As you can see, I am not very busy."

Later that week, Tommy returns to visit his attorney (Ty Van Yen) at his office to learn that it could take a year or two to get the necessary paper-work, and even then, they may say no.

Ty explained to Tommy that there is another way: smuggling him out of Vietnam.

Tommy responds, that sounds risky, how can that work?

Ty – I know of a person who knows people who plan to either take you and the child out by boat or by aircraft. Time of day is not known by anyone except you and captain.

Tommy, Sounds good.

Tommy thought, perhaps it is time to meet the boy, or am I rushing things? He knew he had to pray.

He went to a place near the sea. A place he and Chi would visit quite frequently. He kneeled and began to pray, first ask Jesus for forgiveness of praying to his gods, knowing there should be no other god before Jesus, and Tommy respected that, but he also felt a sense of balance when he spoke directly to Jesus and asking Him for all signs leading to his decision.

There seemed to be a lot of noise during his prayer, what does that mean? However, he continued to pray for hours until he was sure he was doing the right thing. Still not clear on the matter, he stopped praying and began to walk along the water. Taking deep breaths of sea air and still asking Jesus for help. Just then a starfish washed up onto the shore and he thought that it must be a sign. Starfish were a sign for making a difference in the world.

His Gramps once told him a story of an elder from an Indian tribe, walking along the sea and retrieving starfish and gently placing them back into the water. The Elder continue to retrieve starfish and continues to return them to the sea. The Elder is approached by a young warrior, and he ask the Elder what are you doing, and the elder responds, "I am placing these starfish back into their environment so they may have a chance to live.

The young warrior replies, I walk these shores every day and I see thousands of starfish, wash up on the shore, and as the sun reaches its highest point the starfish begin to dry up and die, and with that said, "there is no way you can make a difference."

The Elder reaches down and retrieves another starfish and gently places it back into the sea.

The young brave thinks for an Elder he lacks understanding and begins to walk away.

The Elder responds, young brave, did you see that last starfish I rescued, for that one. I Made a Difference.

Tommy reflects and recalls Gramps' words. No matter how small and insignificant it may appear to others, it doesn't matter,,,,,,,,, it only matters to the starfish.

Tommy believed he had his answer and retrieved the starfish from the beach and placed it back into its environment, and thought, Gramps would be proud of TomTom.

Tommy decided to write a letter to Chi, even knowing he would not mail, but it always made him feel better.

Dear Chi

I know you won't mind, but if all goes well, I am going to adopt a boy whose parents were killed during the battle in Saigon. I don't know anything about him, but sister Grace explained that he is a caring, well-mannered boy. Sister Mary was killed during the last battle in Saigon, she was shot rescuing children from the city streets and passed on a few days later. Her body was put to rest on the grounds out back and everything appeared to need repair.

I always wanted a son. I will find out more about him after I get the necessary papers. I have hired an attorney, Ty Van Yen. I will revisit his office in a few days to learn what he can do.

I wish I knew where you are. Tommy

Knowing from experience how he felt as an orphan gave him a positive answer, and he would start planning. Because of time he decided to fly. Now he needed to sit down with sister Grace and explain to her what was happening.
He wondered how much the boy knew, and whether sister Grace had talked to him.

He learned that she did not mention a thing to him because she did not want him to get his hopes up and then be disappointed.

After a short conversation, sister Grace said, I feel it is time for you to meet Richie (Richard Molland). He was about the same age as Triple T's son, that he doesn't know of.

Being at the home for several years, he learned to speak French, Vietnamese, and English. Richie also enjoyed reading a variety of literature and loved playing basketball. He was tall and had blonde hair, hazel eyes with a tint of blue, he loves music and played the piano. He learned what the sisters could teach him.

Chapter 18
Triple T meets Richie

It was a beautiful day in Ho Chi Men City, and Triple T sat nervously waiting to meet Richie. The room was dimly lit, as the sun's rays provided light to make it feel warm and inviting. Richie entered the room, and sister Grace said, "There is someone I want you to meet, and he has something he would like to explain to you if you are willing to listen."

Richie said, "It would be my pleasure." As sister Grace later explains to TTT, "This is how he was taught to speak when someone asks him to do something. It is a reminder that it is a pleasure to serve you.

Sister Grace introduces Richie to Triple T. Triple T. asks Richie to "sit down or stay standing, whatever way is comfortable." Tommy begins to explain.

"I would like to take you to a beautiful place in the United States to live. This also means that, with your permission, I would like to adopt you as my son."

Richie replies with tears, "How can we make that happen?"

TTT responds, "I tried to go through legal steps to do so, but it seems the government has a dislike for Americans, and we would have to smuggle you out along with me out of Vietnam."

Richie "How?"

TTT, ask Sister Grace if she would please leave the room." Sister Grace responds, "It would be my pleasure," and explains she would stay near-by.

TTT explains to Richie that they would fly out, date unknown, location unknown, but safe. Everything must stay quiet. No one except the pilot will know. You and I will know. Do you understand it must be a secret? Even sister Grace cannot know. Do you understand?"

Richie, "Yes, Sir, I understand."

TTT, "What do you understand?"

Richie, "What do you mean, sir?"

TTT, "You got it."

TTT asks sister Grace to come back into the room. He explains that he must visit his attorney, says goodbye, and assures Richie he will return.

After visiting his attorney, they made an agreement on the cost. Ty explained, "I don't know the name of the person you will meet, and I want to keep it that way."

TTT says, "Okay, I understand."

Ty said, "You will meet him at a place in the city, near here. It is Barba Q and Bar, and he must be paid in cash. USA dollars will work." It would cost him nearly $7,000.00 US, which was fine with TTT.

TTT, ask, "when?"

Ty, "You will receive a message from a stranger, and I don't know when."

TTT waited for a message. Days passed, and on the fourth day, someone on the street bumped into him and secretly handed him a note.

As though nothing had happened, TTT continued to walk, with the note tucked firmly in his hand. When he thinks it is safe, he reads the note that explains to him to meet him at 7, at the BBQ, and I will know who you are.

That evening, TTT is at the BBQ and sits near the middle of the restaurant, where it would be easy for anyone to see. A man who seemed to have too much to drink stumbles into the back of his chair and whispers into his ear, "Meet me out back." The man continues to stumble and exits the BBQ.

TTT waits a few minutes, pays his tab, and leaves. He walks out and waits. About 5 to 10 minutes pass, and he is met by a lady who is presenting herself as a prostitute. She threw her arms around him and explained to come with her. She tells TTT in a soft voice, "Don't get any ideas, if you do, I'll kill you."

She takes him to a place where they could get a taxi, and they get into a cab, and drive a few blocks, and she gets out. Now it is he and the driver. The driver says, "I am your pilot. You and your passengers will meet me at a private air strip outside the city on Friday at three in the afternoon. Act like you are a sightseer, camera, and backpack with what you need. I will let you know where we are flying to when we meet. Understood?"

TTT ", I understand, and thank you."

Smuggling people out of Saigon would be a complex, dangerous undertaking requiring strategic planning.

The communist government-controlled movement within and out of Vietnam was complex.

Land and sea borders were heavily patrolled, and checkpoints made it extremely risky. Escaping by sea, the threat of storms, piracy, and encounters with hostile vessels would be challenging. There was a plan. The pilot explained that air travel would be impossible due to beefed-up security, and he felt he had a better plan, but it would cost them another $5,000.00 each. He had the money in his pocket and asked for the rest of the plan. The pilot explained that he would travel with them by cargo ship to Con Son Island. The island is where prisoners are housed, and the ship's itinerary is to drop off prisoners and then depart for Manila to drop off cargo. He explained that they would be safe in part of the ship used to smuggle others out of and assured them that he would stay with them until they arrived in the Philippines.

TTT hands the captain $10,000.00 in USA currency, and the captain hands TTT $3000.00 back and explains that it will be enough. On the day they are to depart, he arrives at the home to pick up Richie.

He tells Sister Grace, "The less you, the better," and she agrees. When we are safe, I will contact you, or my attorney will. Sister Grace did not know of the plan to give the Christian Home substantial money, and the attorney would explain.

It had to be safe before transferring one million US dollars from his bank to his attorney. He wants the home renamed Chi's Catholic Home for Children Left Behind.

When prisoners are dropped off, the border patrol begins inspecting the cargo and opening all cargo containers. They check the paperwork of all the workers and inform the captain that it is okay to depart. After being at sea, they enter international waters. They let their three passengers out of their hiding place, and they should feel free to enjoy the trip. The pilot and the captain were close friends and shared the captain's quarters for the rest of the trip.

TTT asks the captain if he and Richie could assist in any way, and the captain explains, "You are our guest, and we are here to serve you. Let my first mate take you to your quarters." The place they would share for the next few days was clean and comfortable.

Before leaving the Philippines, he thought he would visit the center for refugees during the war and inquire about Chi. He spoke to several people about Chi Le and heard the same message everywhere he went. Names were changed, and all records were burned for the safety of the refuge. He shared the only photo of Chi he had with him, and some said that it was before I was working here. Some explained they had a high turnover, but to check again, in Honolulu or San Francisco. They may have something more there.

After docking, he and Richie took a taxi to the airport. They couldn't book a flight until later in the week. They would take Philippine Airlines (PAL) from Manila to Honolulu. Richie explains to Triple T. that he did some research on Manila, and suggests they stay at the oldest hotel in Manila, The Manila. A room is booked. Entering the hotel, they see white walls and many arches that seem to be the dominant themes, and it is a great place to dine. Soon after they are in their suite, Richie suggests they visit the National Museum of History. Even though it is within walking distance of the hotel, the doorman suggested they take a hotel jeepney and tip the driver. The jeepney is a unique form of public transportation. Transformed jeeps left behind after World War II are vibrant, colorful, and artistic. No two are identical, and they would look great under disco lights. The driver tells them to ask any employee to call, and someone will pick them up. TTT hands the driver a hundred-dollar bill. They explore the country's diverse flora, fauna, and geological features, including the "Tree of Life," which displays different ecosystems. They find this amazing. The museum houses a variety of specimens, including fossils, and showcases the country's biodiversity.

The hotel is a short distance from many historical places to visit. The next morning, they used a private tourist company to show them all the sites in Manila. They visited Fort Santiago, which offered a glimpse of the past, and they saw the grand Manila Cathedral, a beautiful historic church located in the religious district. They also saw the Case Manila, a Spanish colonial mansion showcasing the lifestyle during that period.

The driver suggests they take a bus ride for a few blocks, as that is the true feeling of Manila. He will follow the bus, waiting for them to exit.

The driver drops them off at a convenient stop, and they board the bus. Triple T. tells Richie, "Perhaps this would be a great way to travel across the USA once we get to San Francisco. Richie says, "It is better than a sharp stick in the eye." TTT laughs and says, "I guess so." They ride on the bus until the last stop because they witness things they may see in Mexico, but not in the USA, unless it is after a sporting event. Tommy felt for many who were on the bus, especially the children, and wondered how their lives would be.

Before leaving the Philippines, he thought he would see the center for refugees during the war and inquire. about Chi. He spoke to several people about Chi Le and heard the same message everywhere he went. Names were changed, and all records were burned for the safety of the refuge. He shared the only photo of Chi he had with him, and some said that it was before I was working here.

Some explained they had a high turnover, but to check again, in Hono-lulu or San Francisco. They may have something more there.

He and Richie boarded a 747, routed to Honolulu, and would soon be on American soil. In Honolulu, he began to call Woody to let him know where he was and to start planning a room for Richie. He explained that he was a 13-year-old orphan whose parents were killed in Nam, and he is now my adopted son. Woody sounded excited and said he would do everything possible to make the homecoming perfect. TTT said, "Please, no band."

TTT then visited an international bank to transfer a million dollars plus ten percent to his attorney. The money was on its way. When Sister Grace met with the attorney and he explained what was about to happen, she fell to her knees, thanking Jesus repeatedly. She asked how Tommy could do this, and Ty explained the story he heard from Triple T. She thought, how can we ever thank him for his generosity, and said to her-self, "Follow through on the plan.

Richie and Tommy land in Honolulu and plan to fly to San Francisco and on to Pennsylvania.

They would stay at the Royal Hawaiian Hotel, a beautiful luxury hotel with great beachfront and dining.

TTT explains to Richie that he must visit the USS Arizona Memorial at Pearl Harbor. He thought, "Would there ever be a memorial built to honor Vietnam veterans?" He read the names of 2043 soldiers lost during the bombing on December 7, 1941. As Richie observed, he saw the anguish in his father's face and knew he had to be a great person with a heart for others and felt blessed that he was with him.

Richie asks his father if they can visit an active volcano, and he says, "If we can, we will." They would also enjoy the beach and all the available water activities. A helicopter tour to visit the volcano the next morning was arranged. The pilot would point out all points of interest while flying to and from the island. The volcano was located on the Big Island, only minutes away by helicopter. Viewing the volcano from the air is a dramatic and breathtaking experience. The vast, rugged landscape with the red-orange lava house in the crater. It was fighting and beautiful beyond words. It was angry as it released gases that exploded and produced smoke. On this day, there was very little overflow emerging from the crater. Thankfully, they had a camera and took many photographs. Richie felt very comfortable with Triple T, and vice versa. Tomorrow morning, they will be heading to San Francisco.

Both travelers were up early and ready to take a taxi to the airport. They were excited that their next stop would be on continental American soil. Richie ensured that Triple T. was packed and ready for their next stage, and they were one step closer to Pennsylvania. They both had their backpacks slung over their shoulders and a few bags of souvenirs purchased for safekeeping.

They anxiously await boarding a 747 to San Francisco. Triple T. tears up, perhaps because he is going home or did not find Chi.

Chapter 19
Homecoming

So much for not bringing attention to you, Woody shows up at the airport in a limousine with a professional driver, who is dressed in black with a hat and tie.

In 1980. Whether on Seventh or Fifth Avenue, New York City is the intersection of decay and survival. The legacy of mid-century glamour had receded into the shadows of boarded-up shops, closed-down movie houses, and strip joints masking the ghosts of once-grand stages. This stretch of Manhattan bore witness to the aftershocks of the 1970s—an era marked by near-bankruptcy, rising crime, and relentless urban erosion. Yet the city did not collapse. It lingered, hollowed and hardened, carrying stories that no longer made headlines.

Behind every blinking neon sign, a laugh once shared outside a jazz club, a whispered argument beneath a marquee that once blazed with a Broadway hit. In this decade, the theaters that had drawn elite crowds were now worn skeletons; They had changed but not forgotten who they were. The asphalt itself seemed soaked in memory.

The limousines driving down Seventh Avenue evoked something fragile, like a whisper from another era. Those who noticed it didn't know why they stared, only that they felt something—an ache, a flicker of recognition, maybe envy. Still, it captured the street's attention in a way no bright sign could.

1980s New York was not beautiful. It was broken, resilient, alive in its stillness. The limousine moved slowly, long enough to see everyone as they moved from store to store. Woody speaks, "Boy, how times have changed. I recall going on a ship with my parents and grandmother. Women dressed in their Sunday's best. Dress with a matching hat, and men in a white shirt and hat." Richie, "Boy, look at the diversity. Everyone is shopping together without guns. Tripe T, "at least, we can't see them." Woody and the driver laugh." Richie, "I guess I can say, 'I'm home." Triple T, "home is nothing like this. Home is freedom to roam and see things most city people never see. Miles and miles of forest, green grass, fields of corn, and you can fish in your backyard. And able to sit in your front yard, without any clothes," Woody and the driver laugh. Richie thinks, I guess that is funny, I find it rude and not a great view of a gentleman.

Once the driver stops in front of the bank, Triple T exits the vehicle and tells the driver, "To take them to eat, tip 20 percent, and add it to my bill."

Triple T. exits the vehicle with a large silver case and the a key marked 743 to open the inherited safety box. He enters the bank and approaches the lady sitting at the desk, asking, "Can I see deposit box 743?" The clerk responds, "743, that must be an old box." Triple T hands the teller some paperwork showing that he inherited the box's contents.

He enters the vault with a person with the other key, and they open a large box 743 together. He thought that it was a large box. Simultaneously nervous, He slowly opens the box and discovers 100,000 dollars of gold coin, diamonds, precious stones, savings bonds, and many other investments he knows nothing about. He found that he owned the building he was standing in and thought it must be worth millions. Before he leaves, he reads most of the papers and places all the documents into his briefcase for his attorney to review and moves toward the exit. The most remarkable thing he noticed, was a note saying, "whoever opens this box is the sole owner of all my wealth.

Remember, share what you have, and keep me in your thoughts. Gramps

Tommy wonders why his attorney never told him what was in the box; it was simple; he didn't know, only the person who opened the box would.

Tommy returns to the limousine and asks the driver to "drive to the Empire State Building."

"Yes, sir," replies the driver.

Triple T "Well, Richie, it is time to start filling in the blanks on your bucket list, and our first stop is the Empire State Building." Richie's eyes show joy, happiness, and excitement, just like a 4-year-old in a candy store, toy store, or an ice cream parlor. Richie Joy is bubbling over. He looks at Triple T. and says, "Thank you. Did you know a secret balcony is only accessible by a steep metal staircase behind a locked gate?"

Triple T. responds, "Yes, and informs Richie and Woody that their driver, Gus, made arrangements for them to experience the VIP tour. That would take them to the 103rd floor to see the 360-degree view of the city. Now we can put that camera to use. We will sleep at The Ritz-Carlton tonight, and tomorrow will come, but let us live today. After what you have been through, you deserve it."

As they arrive, Gus makes a call, and within seconds, Jay, our tour guide, greets us with a smile and says, "It is my pleasure to be your Ambassador on your VIP tour to and above the main floor of the most significant building in the world.

Jay begins the VIP tour with the red-carpet treatment. As they enter the building, he points out the significance of the popular Art Deco design of the time. The building was built for forty-four million dollars in 1930 and only took 13 months.

Note "the bold and vivid colors." He continues as Richie takes it all in and thinks this is much better than reading about it. He points out the luxurious materials, such as gold, marble, velvet, brass, and chrome, which add to its flamboyant chevrons and style.

After a brief stop at the 5th Ave lobby, it is off to the 86th and 102nd-floor views of the city. Triple T. thought about an orphan boy who was blessed in many ways and thinks about Gramps and his philosophy. He thinks about war, love, and his blessings. All he can think about is how much he wishes Chi were there.

Has he thought about war? His thinking is amplified – there are no winners, but a hell of a lot is lost. He thinks about the families torn apart by the death of a loved one, and it makes no difference which side you fought for. The loss of a child fills the same. What did we gain? Nothing. The USA, like after every war, will offer much aid to help rebuild, and thought what a waste.

Chapter 20
Ashley

It was early morning, and Trible T. was still in bed. He heard a knock-knock and a voice yelling for Tommy. Woody was at the door, short of breath; Triple T., said, " What is it that could not wait until the sun was up. Woody explains, "that he got a call from the VA Clinic, and Ashaley was trying to contact him, but all she was getting was a busy single," and she said it was an emergency. Triple T. said, "I have my phone off the hook so I could sleep in." He jumped out of bed and said, "Is everyone accounted for?" Woody responds with a strange look, "I believe so." Triple T. "Get the truck warmed up." And within seconds, he is outside in the truck and on the road to see Ashley.

When they got to the Clinic, Ashley was waiting at the door. She began to explain, "I got a call from your commanding officer to contact him; it was about Chi Le." Triple T. started to think that they had found Chi. He recalls talking to General Oparnico a few days earlier and asking him to see if he could locate her.

He called General Oparnico, who was in contact with Admiral Saula, a specialist in finding lost veterans and said they would. The general informs him that they have some information about Chi Le. Sadly, he explains, that Chi Le was killed while trying to escape Saigon."

Triple T. falls to his knees, and in silence, no words could describe the sorrow he was experiencing. Was it anger, or was it guilt, that he did not do enough to find her? Or is it both?

He thinks, "How will I ever move on? She is everything. She was my first and only love; she was the foundation that made me want to live. Before I met her, I wanted to die, lost my parents, lost my Gramps, didn't understand why, I turned to Jesus, did I lose him?" He reminds me every moment of everyday that I must be strong for Richie, Woody, Maddog, and The Marshal. Life will go on but just let me grieve in peace.

Dearest Spirt of Chi.

I recall the pledge we made to share our lives together, until death do us part. I recall how I explained to you how I would forever support your dreams and desires, needs, and wants. We did build a relationship based on trust, support, intimacy, and closeness. I can feel the warmth of your heart ass I stand in the coolness of the wind.

We accepted our imperfections and celebrated each other's triumphs. He recalls taking you daisy because you loved them, and how you would remove the peddles, one my one, while saying he loves me he loves me not, and when you got to the last two, you would say, "who cares, I know he loves me" and toss the remains into the air.

I haven't spoken to you in many years, yet I feel the warmth of your love as it echoes into the wind. I shall fly like a falcon, build like a beaver, and continue to run like a deer. I will place a black ribbon on each post, and when the sun sets, I will know you are in the world of spirits. Every sound of an owl lets me know you are here.

Forever Love Triple T.

Triple T. always found comfort in writing letters to Chi; it brought him peace and security. Just then, there Woody is standing beside his bed with his hand on Triple T's shoulder shaking him and saying, "wake up your having a nightmare."

Breathing rapidly and in a cold sweat, he feels blessed. He begins to analyze his dream. Was it a message? What was the gods telling me? Was Jesus sending me a message? Who, What, Where, and When? "Woody, please get me a four-wheeler so I can go to the rock, to reflect, and talk to Gramps." Woody responds, "There is one outside."

Tripple T. is dressed and wrapped in an Indian blanket flower or fire-wheel, the scientific name is Gaillardia Pul Chella. It is what he calls his praying blanket. As the sun rises, he kneels on the rock. Facing east with two hands pointed toward the heavens, chanting, or calling for answers, he continues chanting as he waits for the response. The response may come in different ways. The blue bird is strongly associated with hope; they symbolize the essence of life, reminding one of the beauties of nature, and it embraces a positive outcome. It reminds us to hold onto faith. Many animals are a good sign, the dove for peace, the elk for strength, the buffalo for a life of abundance, the eagle for courage and wisdom, the bear for courage, strength, and resourcefulness, the phoenix for rebirth, hope, and renewal.

As he kneeled and chanted to the gods, he felt the cool breeze and smelled the freshness of air. He knew he was blessed as he continued to sing a song from his childhood. *"On the wings of faith, - I rise, soaring high above the skies, - in your love I find my strength, - in you grace I find my length, - wings of faith lift me high, - with your strength I face each day, - In your grace you light my way, - through the trails and storms, - you lift me high."* He believes his mother taught him this song and in his native tong he chants as he repeats, until he receives a sign.

Woody returns to the mountain top and tries to get Triple T's attention. Triple T pauses and speaks, "I see you. What do you want? I believe you got a message by phone, your friend from NYC called, and asked you to call him, it is very important. Triple T. felt disappointed in the gods for not responding to his prayer. He looks toward the heavens and speaks in silence, "I know you are in my presence." He looks at Woody and responds, "Thank you, my friend." As he starts down from the mountain, he asks the gods "to make it good news."

Chapter 21
JJ and Gus

He calls his friend and JJ explains, "I saw Chi, I know it was her, who would ever forget her beauty. I tried to get across 5th Ave to catch her, but she got lost in the crowd." Triple T. knew he had to go to the city and would travel by train; it would be quicker than flying. There was a station 10 minutes from home and he would catch the early train and be in the city by 6:30 am. He would ask Woody and Richie to travel with him. Woody never met Chi, but through Tommy, he feels like an old friend.

Grand Central Station, and Gus is there to meet him, fully dressed in a black hat, black jacket, white shirt, blue tie, and shoes shined to perfection. Triple T informs Gus that they need to pick up T.J. Jackson in West Harlem. Gus responds, "Yes, Sir, while mumbling upscale."

Once they arrive, Triple T, Woody, and Richie go to the front door. Triple T wants to introduce them to his family. T.J. answers the door, sees the limousine, and responds, "You'll fit right into this neighborhood." Triple T introduces them to T.J., his mother, and his father. They sit down, and Triple T explains what he has been up to and the wealth he has accrued. Since T.J.'s call, he has begun to breathe again.

They plan to go to 5th Avenue and visit as many shops as possible with a photo of Chi to see if anyone recognizes her. They will also visit the police and other places of interest. They will leave a photo and a calling card. While at the immigration office, a supervisor said she looked familiar, but he wasn't sure. Triple T thought our first lead was better than nothing. He thanks the gods and asks Gus if he knows a sketch artist. Gus responds, "There are many artists in this area."

Gus makes a few calls and says, "Let's go. I believe I found what we need. The name of the place is Lost—I'll find them." The shop is a few blocks south. When they arrive at the shop, they meet a man named Undercover. Triple T goes into the shop with Gus and shares the photo. He explains that the picture was taken about ten years ago. Can you add a few years? "Yes, sir."

Undercover takes the photo into the back of the shop and, within 15 minutes, has an updated photo: "I believe she would look closer to this." Triple T. responds, "She is more beautiful than ever." They stay in the city for three days, and every place they go turns out to be another dead end.

Triple T confesses, "Until I die, I will never give up trying."
"I think it is time we head home."

Dearest Chi,

The last three days have been an adventure. We spent time in The Big Apple, because someone said they saw you shopping. We went from shop to shop with a photo and only one person said they thought it was you. We had an artist modify your old photo to look more like you today, and you are more beautiful than ever. I will never give up looking for you.

Love Triple T.

Triple T. looks at Gus and asks, "are you available to drive us home, and I will pay you well." Gus responds, "It will be my pleasure."

Triple T. ask Gus, "are you married," and Gus said "yes, we have two children, Lamar and Joan Marie, they are twins." Triple T. responds "Perhaps they may want to join us. Gus, "my wife works as a waitress and our children are in school." Triple T. responds, "perhaps next time."

As they were crossing The George Washington Bridge Triple T. takes in the magnificent view of the Hudson River as it captures a panoramic view of the beautiful ski line that will be tattooed to his memory forever. He admires the impressive steel towers and speaks up to let everyone know that all that steel most likely came from Pennsylvania. Gus follows I-80 west.

After arriving home, Triple T. explains to Gus. "I would like you to become my personal driver. The new company car of his choice is in our company's name, a $ 1 million retirement fund is set up in your name, a new home is built on our property, and $30,000 a year, plus health care. Please talk it over with your wife and family before making a life-changing decision," Gus thought, "is this a cult or is this just a nice guy?" Everything he experienced made him believe that this was just a great man. Their agreement includes living by the code. Gramps rules.

Chapter 22
Back to NYC

Triple T. decided to travel back to NYC and visit 5th Ave again. He wanted to spend some time with Undercover. Once back in the Big Appl. He asks Gus if his family can join him for dinner this evening and where they would like to go. Gus responds, "Emperor Dumpling on 6th Ave. How does that sound?" Triple T. responds, be ready at 6:30 I will have a car sent around to pick you up. I will make all arrangements from the concierge desk.

The car is there exactly at 6:30, The driver opens one door, and Triple T. opens the other door. Before getting into the car Gus introduces his wife, Yvonne, and his children Lamar and Joan Marie. Once they get to the restaurant, they are all seated, and Gus begins with small talk asking Lamar if he is a Yankee's fan and he responds, no, I like the Mets. Good replies Triple T. Let's see if we can get some tickets. He then asks Joan Marie what she likes, and she says, shopping and Broadway. Triple T. what would you like to see on Broadway. How would you like to see The Phantom of the Opera, or 42 Street, I know they are both playing. Woo responds Joan Marie, and I bring a girlfriend, yes if Mom and Dad agree. I believe my mom would also enjoy either. Triple T. "is this weekend okay." Mom, what do you think. "Yes." Triple T. "I'll make arrangements."

Larmar asks, "can I bring a friend, "if you don't mind your dad and me joining you." "Great" replies Larmar.

Yvonne "did Gus mention my proposal?" "Yes, but I have to be sure this is the right move for our family." "Of course you do, I would like for you to visit our home." Yvonne responds, "That would be nice, let's come up with a plan?"

Triple T. makes all the arrangements including limousine service for the ladies, dining at Sardis in the heart of the Theater District, it has been the toast of Broadway for many years., it will be a night to remember forever.

The boys will go to see the Mets vs Pirates play, Triple T. as been a Pirates fan as long back as he can remember. He will never forget 1960 when the Pirates beat the Yankees. All in all, it was a night to remember, the Pirates won.

Triple T. goes to meet with Undercover. He explains his situation with Chi Le and explains that he would do most anything to find her. Undercover explains that there 75,000 Vietnamese women living in NYC. Triple T. goes on to say, "she is 30 years old, 5', 10 inches with hazel eyes, beautiful black hair, that came down to her knees, speaks many languages and is extremely intelligent. Her smile would light up a room." Undercover responds, "that may bring it down to less than a hundred, now we have something to work with."

Undercover gets on the phone and begins to get the word out and offers $5000. dollar reward for information that lead to finding Chi Le. The government phones begin to ring off the hook. "Looking for a Vietnamese woman who is 30 years old, name changed, from Chi Le, etc. The underground communication system has contacts all over the state. Underground tell Triple T. "If she is in the city we will find her." He then tells Triple T. my initial fee is $10,000 and my fee can vary from 50,000 upward, plus expense. Triple T. hands him an envelope with $15,000 and tells him to keep the change. He exits the shop, he SAYS "call me, when you got something."

Two days passed, three days passed and on the fourth day he got a call from Undercover. Undercover explains, "we have narrow it down to less than 30 women, all named Chi, all 30 years old, all bored in Vietnam. she has got to be in this group, call me tomorrow or stop by the shop."

Triple T has Gus pick him up early the next morning. They go directly to see Undercover. He explains we have it narrowed down to three women, and we know more about each of them. Triple T. is any of them a Catholic Christian? "I'm not sure responds Undercover.

In the meantime, Chi is informed by her social worker that someone is looking for her. Instantly she thought I must leave the city. She and T. Le get on the next train to Philadelphia to meet an agent who will take them to a safe house, until they can check things out and make sure it is safe for her and T. Chi Le has tremendous fear because of she saw in Vietnam. When it comes to her safety, she doesn't trust anyone.

They board the train at Grand Central, she knows they are being watched, her and T. have a plan to get off the train in Treton NJ. Chi feels this is a busy stop and they could get lost in the crowd. T. tells his mom he is going to the restroom, a few minutes before they stop. Once they stop, she leaves a small bag on her seat and starts walking with the crowd towards the exit. Acting as though she is looking for T. once at the exit she seems to bend down and walk with the crowd. Acting like she got of the train, while continuing to stay down to the next exit where she gets off. She now has a ball cap and a different jacket and she is lost in the crowd.

Once off the train she sees T. dress in Eagles gear and heading toward the main exit. Chi is also dressed in a different outfit, as they meet outside the station. Chi starts walking back toward the ticket counter and purchases one ticket to Chicago, and shortly after T. purchases a ticket. They will travel to Chicago and meet at her friend's house.

Chi is now dressed to look like an old lady, with gray hair, a walking cane, darker skin, and sunglasses. Chi has a jogging suit and long coat that covers her knees. T. is dressed like a normal boy going to college at Northwestern. Two days later they meet at Chi's friend's house in Chicago.

Chi's friend takes them to a home across town where she believes they would be safer. T. is no longer use to his freedom being taken from him and goes out to a local playground to play basketball. When he returns home, he is greeted by his mother, who explains to him, "if you get caught you will know what freedom is!"

Undercover explains to Triple T., "I believe they are in Chicago." We saw them on camera at the train station," "What do you mean they?" "She is traveling with a student, they seem to meet up every two days at a different location, I believe he is a student at Northwestern."

Triple T. "I will get a flight to Chicago." Undercover says, "No, I will, I know what I am doing, please let me do my job, I have eyes and ears on the ground already. and we will find them." Triple T. responds, "I believe you are right; I just hate to sit and wait." Undercover, "I understand."

A few days have passed and Undercover calls Triple T. "It appears they are hiding from you or someone, every we get close the seem to go deeper into the underworld." Triple T. explains, "In Vietnam she was forced to run and trust no one. she experienced things no one would ever want to see, she saw her parents beheaded and was on the run ever since, but I still don't know who she is traveling with."

Undercover tracks down her friend in Chicago, however she says, "she never saw the person they are looking for, and closes the door." "Undercover's agent, from outside the door says, "If you see her tell her Triple T. is looking for her." The door opens, "who did you say is looking for her?" "Triple T." "I don't know any Chi or Triple T." She closes the door.

Undercover calls Triple T. "I believe we are closer than ever and continues to explain the situation with the person in Chicago, and wonders why she open the door, the second time if she didn't know Chi." Triple T. "she knows Chi and I am coming to Chicago. I'll see your contact tomorrow." Undercover, "I am going with you. we don't want to miss her this time"

Triple T. would have Gus met him at Grand Central and drive him to the airport. Two First Class. As he sits on the plane he thought of a song he recently heard, Reunited by Preachers and Herb.
We never broke up, we just been forced apart, I regret the moment I left you alone, we had no quarrels. "I know that I love you because I need your tough. reunited and it will feel so good. All he kept singing was *"reunited and it feels so good."*

In 1985 T. would be 12 years old, Chi is 35 but could pass for a teenager. Undercover and Triple T. met with one of Undercover's contacts. He explains that they were last seen near the campus of Northwestern. In the meantime, Chi does not feel safe and thinks of what her next move should be.

Chi calls her social work in New York City. Darlene answers the phone, and hear a very soft voice, "this is Chi," Darlene asks for her ID # and Chi responds, "3037." Darlene asks, "where are you and what can I do for you?" Chi. "I'm in Chicago. and I need help, they know where I am." Darlene, "Who knows where you are at?" Chi, "the NVA, (North Vietnam Army)." Darlene, "How do you know it is the NVA? Chi. "they were questioning my friend Carol, and she said the looked foreign, please help me." Darlene, "Is your son with you," Chi, "yes!" Darlene, "How close to the train station are you," Chi "not far. We could be there in ten minutes." Darlene, "Have your son call me when you get there, and don't talk to anyone." Chi, "OK".

Chi and T. take a cab to Union Station, Chi calls Darlene and hands the phone to T. Darlene asks T. "is your mom ok, she appears to be paranoid." T. "I know she is worried, but I think paranoid she is not. She is very logical and concerned about our safety. She is very strategic and after what we went through I can understand why." Darlene, "I called her friend Carol, and after our conversation, I feel confident that your father is looking for her. I hope to see you both in the morning." T. "what makes you think it is my father." Darlene, "How many blue-eyed half native Indians, over six feet tall do you know? I'll bet my career on it; this is your dad."

Chapter 23
Reunited

T. and mom board the train, they find a comfortable place to sit, after they get settled, Chi looks at T. and asks, "What did Darlene want?" T. "she believes the man who is looking for us is my dad." Chi, "what makes her think that?" T. "she asks me, how many blue eyed, 6 ft plus, half native Indian men do I know." Chi, "could this be Tommy?" Chi gets tense, and stops talking, this is how she gets when she wants to think.

Chi will have time to think there are 20 stops between the windy city and the big apple. Chi thinks are my nightmares over or is it just beginning? Will he still love me, and she remembers his commitment. We hadn't been together for over ten years; all I could do to stay sane was to write letters that he never received. I trust him with my life, and I am convinced I will wait for him until the day I die. He is my only love. I am a positive person and always try to look at the bright side of life, however, the last 20 plus years have been difficult, but she tried.

She hears next stop Toledo and dozes off until she hears Erie. The ride will take more than 24 hours, giving Chi. a lot of time to think. She looks at T. and sees him sleeping, like he has no worries, and he usually doesn't. She thinks will we ever get back to normal, and immediately her thoughts go to (what is normal?) I want to feel comfortable with who I am, where I am, who I'm with. To me that is normal. (Comfort). Chi dozes off and begins to dream. She sees Tommy and begins to run towards, but when she gets there, he is not there, but she is lost in a jungle and can't find her way out. The jungle is hot, muggy and outright miserable. Once again she sees Tommy and begins to run towards him but when she gets there, members of the North Vietnam Army are waiting for her. They drop her into a deep hole and begin to feel it with dirt, she is standing in the hole and crying for Tommy, the dirt is now up to her chin, and T. wakes her up, "Mom, you are dreaming." Chi puts her arms around T. as she says, "you are my life."

As T. is hugging his mother, she ask Jesus for help. "Dearest Jesus please guide me in the right direction; I feel lost in a world of distrust and anger." She think about her father explaining to never go to bed while you are still angry, and do not give the devil a foothold, and to share with those in need. "Share what. I have nothing." The Lord responds, "You have your wisdom."

She recalls from the book of Proverbs – "Wisdom is the principal thing; learn wisdom and it will give you understanding." Chi was always taught that learning would give her a deeper pathway to understanding, and she responds, "Jesus, I trust you and with all my heart and soul I lean on you to guide me. I will use my learning and combine it with my faith. You have shared your wisdom, which has offered me knowledge, which has given me understanding."

She hears the next stop is Grand Central, she looks at T. and says, "We will walk with no fear, for Jesus is here."

T, "Let's not go back to the apartment until after we see Darlene," T. responds, "sounds like a plan." They board the subway and head toward the Bronx. As she steps from the subway, Chi trips and hits her head. Before you know it, she and T. are in an ambulance heading to the city hospital. She is unconscious, and the staff is taking all precautions to keep her from dropping into a deep sleep. They keep talking to her, and she continues to mumble.

T. is waiting in the waiting room as Darlene arrives. T. explains to Darlene that she fail as she got off the subway and hit her head. She is unconscious and all she does is mumble. Darlene asked T. "Did you eat anything?" T. "I'm not hungry."

WAR, LOVE AND FAITH

A doctor comes to see T. in the waiting room. "I'm Dr. Porcher. I am your mother doctor. She is improving, but we had to stitch her up, and I promise, no scar. I'm good at what I do. She is waking up slowly. Do you have any questions?" T. "Not Now, perhaps later, sir. Thank you."

In the meantime, Triple T. and Undercover land, there is a car waiting for them, along with Undercover contact Dino. Dino explains that "we found her, she had an accident and is in the city Hospital." Triple T. looks at his driver and says, "let's go to the City Hospital."

Once they arrive at the hospital, Triple T. goes to the front desk and asks, "to see Chi Le." The receptionist looked through her log and responds, "there is no Chi Le in our log-in. However, let me check on something." The nurse calls the waiting room where T. and Darlene are waiting and ask T. to come to her desk. T. responds, "I will be right there, thank you mam."

The nurse asks Tommy and Undercover to wait in the waiting room. T. arrives and the nurse ask him if his mom use to be Chi Le, "Why" ask T. "Do you see those men waiting in the room across the hall, they are looking for a Chi Le, and the tall good-looking man with those blue eyes, that could melt the heart of any lady, and his hair braided in a long pig tail, appears to be in love with Chi Le." T. looks across the hall, he sees his father for the first time. He tells the receptionist, "I check and see."

T. walks into the waiting room and slowly approaches, Triple T. with his eyes tearing up and saying, "I believe you are my father, Chi Le is my mother, and she as talked about you as long back as I can remember."

Triple T. looks at T. and he instantly knowing T. is his son, as he slowly drops to his knees, crying and chanting, "I have a son, a son, I have s son." He grabs T's hand and pulls him toward the floor. Huggy him and kissing his chic and thanking the gods and Jesus. Triple T looks at T. and ask, "how is Chi." T. says, "Sir or should I call you dad? According to her doctor she is slowing waking up, she has some stiches, put the doctor promises no scar, he is good, now we wait." He looks at Undercover and says "thank you" have the driver take you wherever you wish to go, I will be around tomorrow or the day after to see you, I will call, let the driver know I will be here and to return after he drops you off."

Triple T. looks at T. and says, "Dad will work. let's go see mom"

Chi is waking up, she doesn't know where she is at, she doesn't know who she is, she doesn't know T. nor Darlene, she looks at Triple T. and thinks this is a dream, but I never cried in my dreams before, her face lights up, tears in her eyes, a smile that show her beautiful white teeth and say, how could I ever forget, you, ------ I love you Tommy."

Chapter 24
Coming home

About a week ago, Gus informed Triple T. that he would take his offer, but it would take time to make all necessary arrangements.

Triple T. calls Woody, "I found her. We are coming home. Please talk to Gus and see if he can come to the city to pick us up. You come with him and furthermore, bring Richie; Woody, you can ride Shotgun. "No problem," responds Woody.

Woody begins to decide and asks Richie to make some space for T. to put things in the bathroom and thinks "I guess they will have to get along; they are brothers." Woody tells Richie, "You will have to share the bathroom with T, T. is the son that your dad never knew he had. He found Chi and is bringing her home." Richie, "No problem, I will make room for him." Woo! thought Richie, someone to talk to, a friend."

Richie is looking forward to meeting T. and Chi, perhaps once again a family. He thinks "not that I don't have a family with Triple T., Woody, Mad Dog, No Teeth Holmes and the Marshal, but it would be much better with a brother and Chi."

Richie has been taught to call men Mr. or Sir. He has always referred to Woody, as Sir Woody, and so on Sir. Holmes, Sir Marshal. and Sir Williams.

Chi is released from the hospital and ask Triple T. to go with her to the Bronz with her and T. It would be my pleasure; responds Triple T. Gus is there to meet them and takes them to the Bronz.

Richie and T. seem to be hitting it off as they talk about sports, music and the things teenagers talk about. Gus tells them, would you like to meet my son Larmar, he is your age and perhaps can show you the city. The boys respond, "Great."

Chi is now in the car, and they are off to Bronz. Chi wants to spend this time with Triple T., but does not want to ignore T. Woody tells Triple T, he will take care of everything, and the boys will see what teenagers do in the city. He explains that Gus has a son their age and he and Gus will look after the boys, and he will call Chi's home in the morning. Chi shares her phone number.

Triple T. looks at Chi, and says, "If this is a dream, please don't wake me up, I have been looking for you for many years, I wrote you letters that you never received, I've traveled around the world to fine you, I spoke to many people, some had good information, but most did not. I would have spent all my money on finding you. I missed the warmth of your heart, the touch of your hands, how you placed you cold feet on my body as we laid in bed, our time in church, just wasting time walking through the park, and so much more, Please don't wake me up.

Chi replies to Triple T. "I know how much you missed me, because of how I missed you, you always gave me hope, and made me feel important, you never looked down on me, you accepted me for who I am, you embraced what I believe in, you kept me safe, yes I've been through hell, but thinking about you and writing letters gave me hope. Being reunited is the greatest gift in the world. Can we still build a life together. You gave me a son, and I would still like to give you a daughter or two. Can we try?

Triple T. "yes, if you're up to it we can start tonight."

Chi "that is what I was hoping you would say."

They embrace and just continue to hold one another tenderly, until they arrive at Chi's apartment.

Once inside, Triple T. asks Chi to sit down. Chi sits down and Triple T. speaks. "Thanks to my Gramps, and Mr. Tucker, I am a very rich man, I mean, we are very rich. We also own a business that is profitable, and supports many families, who share the profit. I've always felt that is the right thing to do. Gramps always reminded me to share what I have. In Matthew 5:16describes Christians as the light of the world, called to share their good news and faith with others, my good news is what Gramps left me. and I want to help as many people as we can. Are you with me?"

Chi responds, "until death do us part."

Triple T. explains what love means to him. love is freedom, and when I look at you, I see love, for you are love. You have become love because you put no barriers between us. No roadblocks, therefore, it is unconditional, and that is why it is freedom.

Chi, speaks, how could I not love you. Jesus sent you to save me. I hated working as a bar maid, where everyman wanted more than food and a beer. No matter what I tried I would always have men trying to touch me, until they heard of me throwing men from the bar. The word got out, she is no one to mess with, and they would leave me alone.

Triple T. "Does that mean you want me to leave you alone tonight,"

Chi, "Just try. and I toss you out of the house."

Chapter 25
Settling In

Gus and Yvone's move into their new home, built close to Triple T. toward the lower part of the mountain. Their home is a four-bedroom. four baths. Built halfway up the mountain. Chi and Triple T.'s new home is under construction, not too far from Gus. It will have at least six bedrooms and bathrooms to match. Chi is expecting a child.

T., Richie, Larmar, and Joan Marie (JM) are attending Shawnee Valley High School. They are all in the 9th grade and seem to enjoy going and coming from school together. The boys are always teasing JM, but she handles it well by saying nothing.

Triple T. explains that Gus can take them to school every day, and T. responds, "We don't need that hype, we just want to fit in.

The boys are involved in sports, and JM is in the band, theater, and glee club, where she is the lead vocalist.

The three boys become standouts on the court. Larmar is noted for his ball handling and his ability to score from beyond the arc. Richie is noted for his defense, but he is also great when he wants to drive toward the basket. He loves to pass off to T., who is great all around. They play freshman ball and go undefeated, but in high school it is the varsity that counts. They go on to play JV their sophomore year and dress for varsity. The coach knows they are better than any of their varsity teammates but doesn't want to start them. He feels he would perhaps destroy them, the last five games of the season, he puts them on the court and the fans love their play and their attitude on and off the court. They have won 3 of the last 5 games, and they are looking forward to next year.

Joan Marie takes her talent to the stage, and lands the lead role in Evita, and she knock the house down when she sang "Don't cry for me Argentina."

On December 19, 1983, Chi and Triple T. became the parents of a baby girl. They will name her Natalie Grace. Natalie is a good Christian name. The name means "birth of the Lord," which is directly tied to the Christian celebration of Christmas. It is also associated with Saint Natalie from both Eastern Orthodox and Roman Catholic faiths. Natalie is a fitting name for those with a strong Catholic Faith.

Chi and family are settled into their beautiful 7-bedroom 8-bath home on Shawnee Mountain in Pennsylvania, between Altoona and Johnstown Pa. Chi second girl was born on June 22, 1985, and they name her Irene. Meaning "peace," the name is associated with Saint Irene. Irene is derived from the Greek goddess Eirene.

In June of 1990 – Tommy T., Richie, Larmar, Joan Marie graduate from high school and Triple T. and Chi have a celebration for them and the entire community. Two years ago, Triple T. Woody, Holmes, Marshal, Williams and along with the Amish constructed a community center that will seat over 300 people, ideal for a large gathering. It is advertised as a BYOB as they explain the party is for high school aged adults. When the food is displayed on the serving tables, there is lobster tail, jumbo shrimp, crab legs, scallops, steaks, chicken, all grilled to perfection, there are egg rolls, Scheie, and a variety of Asia dishes. Most likely dishes most attending never ate or could never afford. They had three bands from New York City, and to tap off the celebration, a firework extravaganza to be set off at 11:00 pm, from the top of their mountain. The 30-minute Firework, extravaganza lights up the skies, and were told that they were seen in Pittsburgh, some 100 miles away.

Chapter 26

Return to Saigon – Ho Chi Minh City – January 2001

Triple T. and sister Grace are arranging the dedication of the Chi Le Home for Lost Children. Over the past 20-plus year Triple T. and his with his attorney have been financially supporting the Chi Le home. Chi Le knows nothing about the home, because Triple T. was waiting for a safe time to travel back to Saigon. His plan includes Chi and him traveling alone and arriving four days before the dedication. Their family and friends will travel, on a rented plane to Ho Chi Men Airport, directly from Johnstown Airport. Here is a list of some who will be joining them in Vietnam. Jacob, Luke, T. T's wife and child, Richie, wife and child, Larma, wife and child, Sir Woody, Sir Marshal Sir Willams, Sir Holmes and their family, Ashley from the VA. Darlene, Undercover, Sue is a waitress, Jackson family from New York, Fox family from LA. He hoped he did not miss anyone.

When Chi and T visit, all signs are covered in black, and Chi starts thinking they are attending a funeral. She thought perhaps the Pope died and she did know because she was traveling. She was very happy to see the grounds being cared for and the new dorms for students. She asked herself, "Where are the students?" The students were on break. This break is to celebrate the Home that Triple T. began to finance many years ago.

Saturday, January 13. 2001

Triple T. has been planning this event for many years. As Chi and Triple T. arrive at the center on the campus of the Academy. Chi begins to think, this must be a huge celebration. Sitting on stage behind the curtain is all their friends from the states and Saigon. Her and Tommy sit and wait for Sister Grace to walk towards the microphone, and she begins to speak. "I welcome you to the event I have been praying for., and I want to thank Jesus for bringing a special person to me, he was lost, confused, but never willing to give up. He came here in search of someone he loved *(Chi's eyes light up)*, and he found more, but had not yet found her. *(Chi takes a deep breath, this is me and Triple T., but why us?)* I would like to first introduce you to Attorney Ty Van Yen and let him share some words with you.

Ty approaches the microphone and speaks, over 20 years ago this man came into my office wanting to know if he could adopt a child who was an orphan hiding here at the home. At the time it was impossible to get anyone out of the country unless you smuggled them out. That is all the information I can share with you in order to protect certain parties. I would like to introduce you to Mr. Tommy T. Tucker from the United States.

Triple T. approach the microphone. "This journey has been one of faith, I fought in a War that I learned to hate, I met a truly beautiful lady, polished to perfection, she spoke with empathy, elegance and grace for others, her compassion for others can be seen in her actions, she took our unborn child through jungles, mine fields, slept in ditches, didn't not eat for days, found work at jobs that most would consider beneath them. She witnesses her parents being beheaded, she saw women rapped and left to die, she saw children whose ribs penetrated their skin.

After years of struggle, she finally found her way to New Yorks City, she took a job with the government and continued to help others. I would like to take this opportunity to bring my wife, Chi Le Tucker, to the stage.

Chi slowly walks to the stage thinking *"I'll kill him,'* when she gets on stage Triple T. embraces her and says "I have some special guest I would like you to meet, just than the curtain open and her grandchildren, began to run towards yelling Ba, for grandmother and Ong for grandfather. Her friends and family begin to hug her and one by one they move to the front rows of the theater.

Now Chi begins to Cry and think to herself. *"I'll let him live."*

After everyone is settled Triple T. begins to speak, "when I thought I lost you I decided to put our money to good use, and what could be more important than this Home. He looks at Chi and says we dedicate this home in your name. The Chi Lee Home & Academy for Lost Children." This year we will be graduated 63 students, and of them 47 where lost children from all over Vietnam. Chi, this is your night to embrace. It is my honor to introduce you to my wife, my everything, Chi Le Tucker. Chi le approaches the microphone, think what can I say, and she hears a voice, "just tell your story."

"How do you find your way home? Triple T. taught me to listen to the wind, and you will hear the gods and Jesus, light a path for you. As I approached the podium I asked, what shall I say, and I heard a voice telling me "To tell my story. "Yes, I remember that day my life was ripped apart, a 12-year-old girl, losing her parents, home, and lifestyle, because of greed, distrust, and ignorance. Men killing because of what they were taught to believe what was right. I was forced to leave my home through my bedroom window, as my father handed me his wallet and gold watch. I spent the money, and to this day I have his gold wrist-watch, He continued to yell "go see sister Mary at the home in Saigon." To me it felt like Saigon was a million miles away. I have nightmares, but not as many, now I have children, grandchildren, and I know I will live long enough to have great-grandchildren.

Let me tell you about sister Mary. She was soft, yet stern, she was empathic, yet precise, she was soft, kind, loving, and my second mother. She and I would sit up at night, talking about the works of great authors, such as Ernest Hemingway. F. Scott Fitzgerald, Harper, Salinger, Toni Morrison, and Faulkner. Steinbeck and others. I graduated from this Academy with honors. I lived here and worked at a BQ in the city, where I first laid eyes on Triple T., to me it was love at first sight, and when I got to know how his heart spoke it was love forever. Love is something no one should ever play games with. Love could be as soft as a feather and as hard as a knife-blade as it pierces your heart.

If it wasn't for our son T., I don't think I would have been here this evening, he is the wind beneath my feet. Now I have a hurricane that will see me through.

I used to think of the contrast between Heaven and Hell. Hell is War, and Heaven is Love. Upon arriving in America, I noticed that there were no armed military soldiers with rifles, and people were free to walk the streets. Grocery stores had items on every shelf. Church bells, school zones, hospitals. It pains me when I hear people complain about the government. America has the greatest political platform in the world and should be protected at all costs. America has a constitution that guides freedom, and should always be protected against aggression, dictators, protect their veteran's and children, keep education out of government, respect our neighbors and trading partners. A nation of immigrants, built of the people, for the people, by the people. I am proud to be an American, but my heart will always be dear and kind to Vietnam. Folks, I want to thank you for your kindness in joining us here this evening, thank you, and may God travel with you.

Triple T. embraces Chi as she kiss him on the cheek and whispers in his ear. Oh, by the way, "I'm pregnant."

The end:

www.ingramcontent.com/pod-product-compliance
Lightning Source LLC
Chambersburg PA
CBHW052115030426
42335CB00025B/2990